The Best
Men's Monologues
of 1996

Other books by Jocelyn A. Beard

100 Men's Stage Monologues from the 1980s

100 Women's Stage Monologues from the 1980s

The Best Men's/Women's Stage Monologues of 1990

The Best Men's/Women's Stage Monologues of 1991

The Best Men's/Women's Stage Monologues of 1992

The Best Men's/Women's Stage Monologues of 1993

The Best Men's/Women's Stage Monologues of 1994

The Best Men's/Women's Stage Monologues of 1995

The Best Stage Scenes for Men from the 1980s

The Best Stage Scenes for Women from the 1980s

The Best Stage Scenes of 1992

The Best Stage Scenes of 1993

The Best Stage Scenes of 1994

The Best Stage Scenes of 1995

Monologues from Classic Plays 468 B.C. to 1960 A.D.

Scenes from Classic Plays 468 B.C. to 1970 A.D.

100 Great Monologues from the Renaissance Theatre

100 Great Monologues from the Neo-Classical Theatre

100 Great Monologues from the 19th C. Romantic & Realistic Theatres

The Best
Men's Monologues
of 1996

edited by Jocelyn A. Beard

MONOLOGUE AUDITION SERIES

A SMITH AND KRAUS BOOK

Published by Smith and Kraus, Inc.
One Main Street, Lyme, NH 03768

First Edition: October 1997
10 9 8 7 6 5 4 3 2 1

The Monologue Audition Series 1067-134X

Contents

Blackwood

Jocelyn Beard

Based Upon "Loss of Breath," a short story by Edgar Allen Poe

Scene: a crypt, mid-1800s

Serio-Comic

Mr. Windenough: a man entombed alive by mistake, 20–40

> *When his neighbor, Mr. Lacko'breath is also mistakenly entombed alive, Windenough (who has been having an affair with Lacko'breath's wife) takes a moment or two to complain about his situation.*

CORPSE: How can you? How can you? *(The Corpse rises, tearing off the bandage 'round its jaws.)* How can you, Mr. LackO'breath be so infernally cruel to pinch me in that manner by the nose? Did you not see how they had fastened up my mouth? You must know—if you know anything—how vast a superfluity of breath I have to dispose of! *(The Corpse stretches and works the kinks out of his neck.)* In my situation it really is a relief to be able to open one's mouth. To be able to communicate with a person like yourself, who doesn't think yourself called upon at every period to interrupt the thread of a gentleman's discourse.

[(LackO'breath tries to say something.)]

CORPSE: Interruptions are annoying and should undoubtedly be abolished. don't you think?

[(LackO'breath makes as if to reply.)]

CORPSE: No reply, I beg you. One person is enough to be speaking at a time. I shall be done by and by and then you may begin. How the devil, sir, did you get into this place?

[(LackO'breath attempts to answer.)]

CORPSE: Not a word I beseech you! Been here some time myself. Terrible accident! You've heard of it, I suppose, an awful calamity! Walking under your windows some short while ago—about

1

the same time you became stage struck, as I recall; strange business, that. In any case I just happened to be passing under your windows, perfectly innocent, mind you—have you heard of 'catching one's breath?'

[(LackO'breath attempts to reply.)]

CORPSE: Hold your tongue, I tell you! Yes, catching one's breath, well, I caught someone else's! I always had too much of my own. I met Bob—you know Bob, do you not? His box adjoins yours at the opera, I believe. Which puts me in mind, what was your opinion of that perfectly dismal production of *Die Zauberflote?* Dreadful, I tell you, dreadful. I never in my life heard such a caterwauling as escaped that soprano's lips! Your own dear wife was particularly offended by it...I mean...so I have heard...from my own dear Mrs. Windenough. In any case, I met Bob at the corner of the street and the stubborn fellow wouldn't give me a chance for a word—I couldn't get in a syllable edgeways and consequently I suffered an attack of epilepsis. Right there on the street! Bob made his escape—damn all fools! They took me up for dead. Your wife was devastated...I mean...she appeared so at the funeral...the loss of a friendly neighbor can be a terrible tragedy. I was then put in this place. *(Bearing down on LackO'breath.)* I heard every word you said about me. Every word a lie!

Burning Down The House

Jocelyn Beard

Scene: a lavender field in Provence, France

Dramatic
Alex: a man trying to restart his life, 30

> *Alex's Croatian wife, Soja, was killed in Sarajevo nearly three years ago. Since her death he has retired to his family's estate in Provence where he eventually encounters Claudia, an American woman who shares with him a passion for art and the need to begin again. Here, he explains to Claudia why he is finally ready to resume living.*

ALEX: Meeting you, Claudia, has reminded me that I am real. It is my life with Soja that now seems…unreal. I suppose that I never really knew her…I never thought for a moment that she would leave…

[Claudia: Alex, you don't have to tell me this.]

ALEX: No, I do. I want you to understand that what is past, and what is present are separate. I met Soja in Paris, seven years ago. She worked as a waitress in a cafe not far from where I worked. We saw each other every day. We smiled, we exchanged pleasant words, we exchanged phone numbers…it was a very easy courtship. She was…easy to fall in love with. But then, the trouble began in Yugoslavia. Soja would get letters and phone calls from friends and family telling her how awful it was, to live in such fear. Never knowing when the next Serbian attack would come. Many of her friends died in Sarajevo, and her uncle, her mother's brother, committed suicide, as did so many others. As those she loved died, so did little pieces of Soja die. I know that she felt great shame at not being there, with her family. I did my best to convince her that she was so incredibly fortunate to be safe here, in France, but she had stopped listening. And then, the

3

calls and letters stopped coming. The Serbian border was now just thirty kilometers from her parent's village in Croatia. The newspapers here and everywhere screamed at us about death squads, genocide and rape camps. I suppose I knew all along that she would try to go home. This, I forgive her. Not saying good bye, I can not forgive. You must understand, Claudia that for most of my marriage, I felt as though *I* was living under siege. For three years the only thing that Soja and I talked about was Bosnia and Sarajevo. We stopped talking about us and our life together, as if nothing mattered besides the suffering in the Balkans, where people have been suffering for hundreds and hundreds of years. And do you know what? People will go on suffering in the Balkans with or without me. And so I must say to myself: *Au revoir, cherie. Au revoir.* That is what is past. And now you have blown into my life, and I find that after all there is still cause for delight in living the simplest of days...like today.

Cheap Sentiment

Bruce Graham

Scene: the Short Warf Cafe, on the Chesapeake Bay

Dramatic
Giddy Rourke: a screenwriter in exile, 70s

> *During the communist witch hunt of the 1950s, Giddy fled Tinseltown for an obscure life fishing for crabs on the Chesapeake. Nearly thirty years later, he is discovered by an idealistic young director who becomes determined to make Giddy's unfinished masterpiece into a motion picture. Here, two very different generations of filmmakers clash as Giddy reacts to the younger man's sense of style.*

GIDDY: Damn, it's been a long time. Last movie I went ta see was *The French Connection.* Thought it was gonna' be a girlie flick. (Back to David as he moves to the Victrola.) You get what I'm sayin', right? When people go to all that trouble and spend all that money *they wanta' feel good when they walk out. (Music begins: "Sonny Boy.")* Listen to that. Talk about your cheap sentiment—Jesus Christ, Jolson was the master. But my uncle, who was one tough sonuvabitch—I saw him take on three of Capone's guys with a meat cleaver in one hand and a pork roast in the other—he bawled his eyes out when he heard that song. Why—did he care about the kid in the song—Christ no. Like most people, he had a crappy life. He hated the meat business, he hated my aunt—what a heifer she was, shoulda' butchered her. But when we came outta' that Jolson show...he had laughed, he had cried...and I'd never seen him so happy in his life. And even though Jolson was a bastard, we loved him. That's why she's gotta' fall in the water. We take this cold bitch in the first five minutes—she gets in a jam—boom—falls in the water— she makes us laugh. Now she's human, we start ta like her. Then

5

we care about her. *Then we like the goddamned movie and we tell all our friends to go see it and make a lotta' money! (Em x's through the yard, all dressed up.)* Nobody goes to a movie cause of the goddamned "thematic underpinnings." Basic primal emotions, Dave, that's why! Emotions! *(With passion; he sounds more like Irv than Giddy.)* We all have 'em. And if you touch that in your audience—that's our job: make 'em laugh, make 'em cry—then you've done something good.

The Coyote Bleeds

Tony DiMurro

Scene: the 124th Precinct

Dramatic
Hunt: a morally bankrupt detective, 50

> *Years on the force weigh heavily on Hunt. When a murder suspect whom he has illegally detained commits suicide in his jail cell, internal affairs threatens to bring charges against him. Here, the soul-weary Hunt does his best to describe the reality in which he is forever caught.*

HUNT: Who the hell does she think she is? Jesus Christ! Two thousand kids a year die in this City as a result of indirect violence and she's busting my balls over some guy who kills himself in prison after he confessed to a murder. Where was his lawyer? Is she... What's next? The goddamn ACLU through the door. God, I loved this country so much more when Reagan was president.

[MITCHELL: But what do we do now?]

HUNT: You know, I got a beating once when I was innocent and it was for my own good. When I was a kid, one Sunday afternoon, the parish priest, Father Ward, rang our bell and told my father that I had stole money from the collection plate earlier in the morning when I was serving mass. My father called me out on the porch and didn't say a word. He just pointed at me and said, 'Is this the boy, father?' And before the priest could speak, my father gave me a back hand that knocked me clear across the porch. Gave me a beating right on the porch in front of everybody—the priest, the parishioners, the neighbors—everybody. Just started slapping me back and forth off the wall. And I didn't say a word. Didn't cry. Didn't do anything except bounce off the wall. The thing was, I didn't steal anything. It was my brother. But you can bet one thing: my brother never stole from the church again.

[MITCHELL: Why?]

HUNT: Because after my father disciplined me I went upstairs and beat the shit out of my brother. You think this guy killed himself because he was innocent? He was guilty of something. Like the guy with thirty-five priors. Just think of how many crimes are not going to be committed because of this.

The Coyote Bleeds

Tony DiMurro

Scene: the 124th Precinct

Dramatic
Hunt: a morally bankrupt detective, 50

Here, Hunt reveals a glimpse of his tortured soul.

HUNT: If you think this is messy what are you going to do when we walk into the projects and there's a woman on the floor with the top of her head blown off? And you think, how the hell did the top of her head come off? And then you realize that the killer stuck a high powered rifle up her ass and pulled the trigger three times. Three times. You see smoke float around the room and a nearly extinguished cigarette in the ashtray. And you try not to vomit. And you know the killer's still close by. You know that because of the cigarette in the ashtray. Vomit is pouring out of your nostrils all over your uniform, but you don't care because you're thinking, 'This is it. I'm gonna get him.' You don't know the first thing about being a cop until you've run down the stairs in the projects. Knowing that every turn could be your last. Because a guy that sticks a rifle up a woman's ass and blows the top of her head off will hit you between the eyes first chance he gets. And your partner is right behind you, but only now he's not your partner. He's your guardian angel. Your savior because he can see over your shoulder while you're blind with rage. But you know he's there because you can feel his breath on your neck and as long as you can feel that you know you're not alone. There's someone there. Some one who understands. You're not alone. And he watches your back so you can move even faster. And he's more than your brother. Because if you die—a little part of him dies. A part that he can never retrieve. So he'll prevent you from taking a bullet. He'll even take the damn bullet himself. He'll die so you can survive.

Dance With Me

Stephen Temperley

Scene: here and now

Serio-comic
Talbot: A histrionic, self-centered crybaby, 30s

> *Talbot has been cheating on Sally with Daisy, a younger woman who is currently spending a romantic weekend with Sally's lover, Jack. (Got that?) Here, the melodramatic Talbot tortures himself by imagining Jack and Sally together.*

TALBOT: What do you think they're doing right now? They're probably at that motel…

[SALLY: I'm not listening.]

TALBOT: They spent a leisurely day in the country. Now they're thinking where to eat…Or maybe they made reservations at some quaint little inn and they're dressing for dinner…

[SALLY: I'm not listening.]

TALBOT: They've had a shower. She s flat on her back. And he's trying to get it hard enough to cram it inside.

[(Sally jams her fingers in her ears.)]

TALBOT: Don't tell me he's any good at it. Is he? He can't be. Is he? What's he like? You can tell me. I mean, you know us both. Not that I'm asking you to make comparisons. I would *never* do that…To tell you the truth, I don't think I'm all that interested any more. If I ever was. I get too nervous. I get headaches. I get these terrible cramps. Maybe I'm queer and don't know it? I don't feel queer but you can't always tell by that. I don't think I'd much like doing it with Jack, either. I bet he loves to do it. I bet he does it all the time. What? Twice a week? Three times? Four? Every night? Twice a night? Holy shit! Not that I think that means anything. Still, how am I going to hold on to Daisy? Can't be much fun for her. Didn't so much matter with you. You'll put up with anything. I want to look after her; cook for her; clean for her; do her laundry…Does that sound weird? I don't really care if she does want to fuck Jack so long as she comes home to me. They could go off like this from time to time… It could work out very well. To tell you the truth, it's almost a relief. She's happy. He's happy. I'm happy. You're happy. You are happy, aren't you?

Day Break

Nathan Parker

Scene: a motel along the I-40, somewhere in Missouri

Serio-comic
Gil: a documentary filmmaker from Orange County California. Whatever his age, he does not look it.

> *Gil has encountered Matthew, a young writer, in a motel in the middle of nowhere. During a bout of drug-taking, tension flares when Gil makes a play for Matthew's young lover, Fay. When Matthew makes the mistake of asking Gil his age, he receives the following reply.*

GIL: I woke up this morning, right—we were staying at some motel in Texas—and I see these seven guys outside my window, not right outside, a few yards away on the edge of this little park. They're standing in a line doing jumping jacks. That's an everyday activity, right, nothing wrong with seven guys in sweat suits doing jumping jacks. Except, I don't think it's an everyday activity, see, I'm looking at them and thinking—what the *fuck* are they doing? I mean, have you ever paused to think how ridiculous a jumping jack actually is? Back and forth with the legs and clap the hands together. I mean, that's not a normal activity, is it? That's fucked up, man, if you ask me. A jumping jack is not something the human body is supposed to do. May as well smash your head against a wall with extreme force. *(Beat.)* There are so many fucked up things in life that we just take for granted. We don't pause to isolate things and examine them for what they really are. That's how I was when I was your age. I did everything conventional society had taught me to do and without the slightest measure of doubt. But as I got older, I don't know, I started to stop and look at things. Who says because I'm a certain age I have to sit in armchairs and smoke tobacco out of pipes and jingle coins in my pockets. I'm no freakin' grandfather.

12

Day Break

Nathan Parker

Scene: a motel along the I-40, somewhere in Missouri

Serio-comic
Gil: a documentary filmmaker from Orange County California. Whatever his age, he does not look it.

> *Gil surreptitiously reads Matthew's journal and discovers that the younger man has described him in less than flattering terms. Enraged, Gil tells Matthew exactly what he thinks of his writing.*

GIL: I'm going to be honest with you, Matthew. Your writing's no good.

[MATTHEW: What do you mean?]

GIL: I mean it stinks. It's shit.

[MATTHEW: It's not shit. How do you know? You only read a couple of lines...]

GIL: I'm in a position to know these things.

[MATTHEW: Position? What position? You're just some old— you don't know anything.]

GIL: Despite what you may think, Matthew, I know a hell of a lot. I've been around the block. Christ, I've been both ways around the block, man. Forwards *and* backwards. I know the block like the back of my hand. *(Beat.)* Who's really living the lie, huh? You or me? I'm not living a lie. I'm a documentary film maker. Go walk the streets of Orange County, man, they know who I am. They know who you are? *(Laughs.)* Philosophical short story writer? Christ, man. Your life isn't just a lie it's a Fantasy fuckin' Island.

[MATTHEW: I'm not listening to you!]

GIL: You know why you're not going to make it? Guts, man. You ain't got any guts. You're as hollow as a tuning whistle. You want to write about me, you've got to be me. That's what writing's about. Experience. You can't write bout anything without having experienced it. Let's see you snort some blow and chug some Nyquil. Can't do it, can you? You're no writer. *(Beat.)* You said this trip was a test—well, you've simply failed the test, that's all. Think of it as a blessing. Some people don't have trust funds... they don't have the chance to drive across America and find out they don't have what it takes. Now you don't have to waste the rest of your life. You can launch yourself into some other career— what do you feel like doin'? Well, you don't have to decide just yet. Wait 'till you get to Hollywood...

> [MATTHEW: I'm not going to Hollywood.]

GIL: But you're on course for Hollywood, right? NYC. Missouri. Next stop the Hollywood sign.

> [MATTHEW: I'll change course. Start heading north. Go up to
> South Dakota to see the Prairie Dogs.]

GIL: You can't change course.

Dead Or Alive

Karen Smith Vastola

Scene: here and now

Serio-comic
Seth: a man in the mood for love, 40

> *While trying to inspire passion in his fiancee, Seth ponders the problematic nature of panty hose.*

SETH: [Even better.] Whoever invented those things must have been a man-hater

[MARGERY: What?]

SETH: Well think about it. Put yourself in a man's shoe or some other place. You have a date with a woman. A woman you really like, or maybe not. A woman you really have had the hots for a long time, or maybe you just have the hots. I mean the horns are on. You take her to the movies or the theatre if she thinks of herself as one of the more cultivated types. You have drinks and dinner before. You have drinks afterward. Now you've invested two hundred or more for the privilege of this woman's company. You're back at her apartment and you do more talking. You listen attentively, patiently to everything she's had to say, even the nonsense about her number and your number and how numerlogically speaking you're not quite a match. You've bitten your lower lip until its almost bled as you try to hold back your laughter at her description of her own personal angel that will accompany her into the next millennium. You finally have her trust. You try the kiss. It leads to more. Before long you're both entangled. The room echoes with sucking noises, short, panting breaths, popping buttons. You've managed to disentangle her from most of her clothing. You've even managed to disrobe yourself without missing a beat or losing the upward spiral of both of your passions, and then, the final obstacle, her panty hose. A synthetic

15

blend so tightly woven that trying to grab it and pull with your fingers becomes a lesson in smooth surface tension and the absence of traction. And god forbid you try to poke a finger through it and rip it. You'll only end up sending the woman screaming as she rushes off the sofa, towards her medicine cabinet to find a bottle of clear nail polish to "Stop the Run." So you try from the top down, but as you fumble with the tight elastic around the waist you realize its quite possible these panty hose may be vacuum sealed. And if the woman is at all vain about a little protruding belly and she's chosen the control-top version you're dead in the water. You might as well be stranded on a desert island with a can of sardines and no key.

[MARGERY: *(Interrupts speech.)* Why don't you just ask her to take them off?]

SETH: And admit defeat. Never. A yard to the goal line and you ask the woman, the opposing team to carry the ball. To the touchdown! Why, if the seduction can't be complete a man's better off removing himself from the situation, getting dressed and regrouping until a better day, a summer day, sans panty hose.

Death Wears Dancing Shoes

Nannette Stone

Scene: here and now

Dramatic
Frank: a man who has just discovered he has a brain tumor, 80

> *Frank has lived his life with passion and tenacity. The news of his tumor has made him determined to use whatever time he may have left in pursuing life's joys as he here discusses with a photo of his dead wife.*

FRANK: *(Having just awakened, rises from his bed and refers to a silver framed photograph that sits on a night table cluttered with vials of pills and medical reference books.)* Last night I fell asleep in fits wrestling with that word. *Positive.* Funny isn't it? Positive sounds like it ought to be a good thing. I had moved my head around on my pillow until perspective had put the North Star right on top of the larch tree outside my window. The wind began singing your name and a thousand fireflies insisted I waltz you to Florida in quicksilver shoes. You know that in my dreams Amelia, we are always still young. And I woke up knowing that I would not cut the grass today, make my bed or step on the scale. That I would not answer the phone or go back to the doctor at four o'clock. That I am going to have a cigar and a salty cheeseburger. Now don't give me that look of yours. *(He pauses and then directly addresses the photo.)* And a double martini! Today I'm going to pull the top down on the old Plymouth and drive that big banana all the way down to Key West. I want to reel in a sailfish. Peel in the sun. Look for cat paw shells and coconuts—Write a poem in the sand. Breathe in salt air. Breathe. Breathe. I know Amelia. I am already eighty going on ninety. An old old fool. But I want to live. Dad lived to one hundred and two. You were only forty-six. You were always so brave. I can't face death. You always said my cup was half full. What's in the other half Amelia? Trouble? I don't want it.

Double Or Nothing

Michael Ajakwe, Jr.

Scene: here and now

Serio-comic
Frank: a blue-collar brother from the 'hood with no kids, 28

> *Here, Frank recalls his first encounter with Sherry, the woman with whom he has fallen in love.*

FRANK: *(Singing.)* "Love them and leave them… That's what I used to to…use and abuse them…" *(Beat; normal speak.)* Until I met Sherry. *(Savoring the memory.)* I'll never forget it. *(Lights fade to dim. Music fades up low under. It's 2nd Nature's "Base Tone Junkies." At the bar, on the other side of the room, a gorgeous woman, Sherry, 29, is staring at what is now a packed dance floor, nursing a drink and watching the festivities.)* She was just sitting there, all by her lonesome, having what looked like a Screaming Orgasm but could've just as well been a V-8. Now, normally, it ain't my style to ask a babe to dance, 'specially when she's thirty feet away, 'cause if I do and she says no *everybody* in the house is gonna know about *(A guy moves from across the room to ask Sherry to dance. She stares him up and down like he's a Martian, shakes her head and looks away, leaving him standing there in front of the whole room like an idiot. The guy looks at the audience, embarrassed, and attempts to "casually" ease offstage.)* See. That could've been me—an accident waiting to happen. *(Sherry makes eye contact with Frank. Frank looks around, unsure whether she's actually looking at him. He points to himself and she nods, looking away.)* Ya'll see that! Got her cold busted. And she didn't even try to hide it. *(Beat.)* Women…Ya'll think ya'll so slick. And you are. But one thing's for sure—when you wanna let a brother know what time it is, ya'll don't waste no time. *(Beat.)* So, what do ya'll think? Should I "go

18

for it?" Should I "make my move?" Or should I just straight up "bum-rush" the show?" *(Off their looks.)* That means everything I just said. *(To a confused patron.)* What's the matter, ain't never lived in the ghetto before? didn't think so. *(Beat, setting his sights back on Sherry.)* I think I'm gonna go for it. *(Starts for the bar, then stops.)* But if she turns me down, I'm kicking somebody's ass.

The Ends Of The Earth

David Lan

Scene: a hospital sitting room, London

Dramatic
Daniel: a geologist whose young daughter is dying, 30

> *Daniel has recently returned from the Balkans where he had been working on a dam project that was causing unrest in the local population. He has returned to London to be with his wife and daughter, who is terminally ill. In a quiet moment, Daniel reveals the dichotomy that has all but severed his soul.*

DANIEL: No. No, you don't know anything about it. That's not going to happen. And the other thing is…About going back, no. I've been there. I've done that. I've learnt what they have to teach. I'm not going back. Is that clear? Ever. *(Silence.)* There's an old dichotomy. Perennial. You think it's been resolved, put to bed. Then you find it's got up again. It's this. Is God—whatever one means by…in or above, i.e. apart from, separate, outside the world? Or…It sounds like nothing. It drives people crazy. Take evolution. The old arguments. Did God make the world as something separate from himself, clay moulded in his hands, a sculpture of which he's the artist, into which his life was breathed? Or is life God? Life itself. How can I put this?

[CATHY: You put it very clearly. You suspect that you're God and you're checking it with me.]

DANIEL: *(Laughs.)* The same problem crops up in all religions: Islam, Judaism—the Kabbalah!

[CATHY: Now you're gabbling.]

DANIEL: It's so important this. In Elizabethan England…When did the Renaissance truly begin? When the scientists, such as they were, struck the earth with a stick and said here, not in the heavens but here, down here, in the earth, *(Holding his body.)* here, here is where holiness is. Look, does God think it's wrong when I wank? Is he: somewhere out there judging me? Or is the pleasure I feel…Or when I eat delicious food or breathe sweet air or make love to you, or simply am with you, talk with you. Like now. Is that pleasure, this huge pleasure—telling you after all this time, this long silence, this ice age, this death-like anger between us, Cathy, how I feel, how I really, truly feel…It's like, you know, I'm full of light. I'm going to burn with it, burst with it. Cathy! Is this…Is this Him? *(Silence.)* Not that I believe in Him.

[CATHY: Don't you?]

DANIEL: That I think I can safely say.

[CATHY: I think you do.]

DANIEL: Oh, fuck a duck, Cathy. What I'm trying to tell you is that I feel I could do anything. The heavens are open. And if I did it, it, whatever it is, and I did it well, as well as I could, if I did it with love and for the love of doing it and only for that reason…

[CATHY: Did what?]

DANIEL: If I choose to do it…I drink too much? *(He flings out the contents of his glass.)* 'Who shall ascend the mountain of the Lord and who shall stand in his holy place? He who has clean hands and a pure heart.' What is it? What is it? Cathy? What is it?

Event Horizon

Christopher Kyle

Scene: NYC

Dramatic
Mitch: a guy who has just lost his job, 40s

> *When Mitch is fired from a Wall Street firm, he phones his
> estranged son, Eric, and begs him to meet him in Central
> Park at Strawberry Fields. Here, Mitch cautions Eric to aban-
> don his youthful idealism.*

MITCH: I lost my job.
[ERIC: You did? Why?]
MITCH: The firm is looking to build a multicultural workplace and I
guess I'm kind of a monocultural guy.
[ERIC: I don't understand.]
MITCH: Twenty years in that place and I'm out on my ass. I was a
rainmaker, for Christ's sake.
[ERIC: I'm really sorry, Mitch. I know your job—]
MITCH: It meant everything to me. I gave up my chance at a fam-
ily life for those bastards.
[ERIC: I'm sure you'll find something else.]
MITCH: You think I wanna go back to the bottom and start cold-
calling again? Fuck that. No way. *(Beat.)* You know what really
gets me? I used to be with those people—civil rights, affirmative
action. Who knew?
[ERIC: They fired you because you're white?]
MITCH: Of course they did. They were just waiting for a cover like
this Algaetech thing to pull the trigger.
[ERIC: What s Algaetech?]
MITCH: Biotech firm went bankrupt today—don't ask. Listen to me
Eric. You're young; you've probably got a head full of help-thy-
neighbor idealism. Get rid of it. Because when you get to be my

age, you're gonna have to drop your principles one by one, and it hurts, kid. It hurts. Until this morning I was a liberal.

[ERIC: I don't know what to say.]

(Mitch nods and pats him on the shoulder.)

MITCH: In my despair tonight, Eric, in the basement of my pain, I got a sudden urge to come down here to Strawberry Fields. And, funny thing, I started thinking of the lyrics to "Imagine." You know, "Imagine all the people..." et cetera. John Lennon was about my age when he got blown away. Saved him, really. I mean, look what happened to George and Ringo. And Paul. Turned into a vegetarian—let Linda play on his albums. And I got to thinking of my youth and how fucked up everything's gotten since John was killed. I was in law school when it happened—I was gonna do public interest, you know? But it seemed like the whole optimism thing went down with John. So I dropped out and got a job on Wall Street. Until today, I never looked back. *(Pause.)* Anyway, right when I'm about to start looking for my own personal Mark David Chapman, I run into this black guy—don't ask me how—and he says to me, totally out of the blue, he says, "Have you been there for your son?" That just hit me, Eric. Like on TV when they have that thing, "Have you hugged your kid today?" and I think to myself I haven't even *seen* my kid in months. I knew right then I had to call you. *(Beat.)* I don't think we talk enough, Eric.

Family Of Horrors

William Gadea

Scene: here and now

Serio-comic
Boyd: a man who has just murdered his father, 20s and Walter, the vengeful spirit of his father, 60s

> *Boyd has become possessed by Walter's wrathful ghost. Please note that one actor must portray both parts! Have fun!*

> *(The lights come up to a dim level. Boyd enters carrying a knife wrapped in a bloody rag. He unwraps the knife, inspects it for one last time, then covers it again and places it in a garbage bag. He takes off his shirt which is also bloody and puts it in the bag as well. He takes the bag off stage. The lights come up to a normal level. Boyd reenters in a clean shirt.)*

WALTER: Murderer!

BOYD: Who's that?

WALTER: You are! You! You're a murderer.

BOYD: Who's saying that? Why are my lips moving when I hear it?

WALTER: Who do you think it is? Your father. Who you killed.

BOYD: Impossible. You're at the bottom of the lake.

WALTER: Well, I'm back now. *(Walter sings a bar of horror movie music...)* Ooooh-ooooh-oooooh-oooooh!

BOYD: It feels like you're inside me. Like you're speaking through me.

WALTER: Bingo.

BOYD: No, it couldn't be. Ohmygod. I must be losing my mind.

WALTER: No, you're not.

BOYD: I must be developing a split personality. Ohmygod, I'm cracking up!

WALTER: Boyd, listen to me: you're not crazy. You're stupid, ungrateful, incompetent and lots of other things but you're not crazy.

BOYD: That's just what Dad would say. Okay. This is probably perfectly normal. I bet even well-adjusted people find killing their father stressful. All right. I give up.

WALTER: All right. I give up. *(Walter starts acting crazy. He makes faces…)*

BOYD: What are you doing?

WALTER: You're crazy, remember?

BOYD: Stop it! Stop it! *(Walter slides his hand down the back of his jeans. Boyd reacts as Walter gooses him.)* Enough! It's you. It could only be you. If I were going crazy I wouldn't be so goddamn perverse about it.

WALTER: Thank you.

BOYD: You're back. To terrorize me. Just like you did in life!

WALTER: Oh, boo hoo. I bet you want to have a good cry now.

BOYD: You're inside me. This is so disgusting!

WALTER: And I haven't even started. I'm gonna make life hell for you, Boyd.

BOYD: How?

WALTER: Just wait and see.

BOYD: I killed you! I'll always have that. I'll always have that look on your face when I came at you with the knife.

WALTER: I never thought I'd see such an ugly side of you, Boyd.

BOYD: What are you talking about? It was your fault. If you hadn't threatened to write me out of your will you'd still be alive.

WALTER: So that's what it was, huh? Money.

BOYD: No, it wasn't just the money. If you'd given me anything else—love, consideration, respect—I wouldn't have cared about the money. But I'll be damned if I'm left with nothing!

WALTER: I think I like the money explanation better. This other one's a little weepy. Boo-hoo.

BOYD: Mock me if you like, Dad. I'm not the one who's dead.

WALTER: And I'm not the one that's gonna wear the funny striped suit.

BOYD: What? Get caught? No way, I've thought of everything.

WALTER: The perfect crime, huh?

BOYD: You're damn right.

WALTER: When they call and tell you I'm missing I suppose you'll pretend you're grief-struck.

BOYD: Yes! I can do it too. My background in acting will finally pay off. It's called an affective memory. I'll remember when my dog Dinkie died and they'll think the tears are for you. Here, let me demonstrate. Officers! Hello. What can I do for you? Well, of course. I hope it's not bad news. What? My father? You don't think… *(Boyd starts chewing the scenery. Aside…)* —this is when I'm thinking of Dinkie— *(Boyd starts sobbing uncontrollably.)* No, no, no! No, no, no!

WALTER: Yeah, but you see, I'm a pretty good actor too, Boyd. You wanna see my impression of you? Officers, officers! I killed him because he didn't love me. Wah, wah!

BOYD: You wouldn't. You bastard.

WALTER: You can bet I won't be in your body when your room-mates redecorate your asshole!

BOYD: *Bastard!!!*

(Walter and Boyd start to fight. They wrestle, pull, slap and punch at themselves.)

WALTER: Outta my face, you moron.

BOYD: You mean my face!

WALTER: Stop it! This is idiotic!

BOYD: I'm only sorry I can't kill you again, you bastard! *(Boyd judo flips himself onto the floor.)* Owww!

WALTER: You satisfied? *(Walter picks himself up.)* Don't get this body hurt. I'm gonna need it.

BOYD: You're gonna need it?

WALTER: Yes. You don't think I'm going on with this charade for ever, do ya? I can't stand your company any more than you can stand mine.

BOYD: So you'll leave?

WALTER: No, you'll leave. You'll take my place in hell and I'll get a few more years here in your body.

BOYD: Oh, no you won't.

WALTER: I just told you, I'll make you get caught, Boyd. I'll make life hell for you. You might as well go to the real hell and start getting acclimated.

BOYD: No, I'm not giving you anything.

WALTER: So you'd rather spoil it for both of us?

BOYD: Yes. Why do you want to take over my body, anyway? You always said I was a sloucher—scrawny—sissy-looking!

WALTER: It depends on how you carry yourself.

BOYD: If I let you have my body you'd ruin it—cigars, rich food. Soon you'd look like the tub o'lard you were when I killed you!

WALTER: I wasn't fat, I was husky. Anyhow, that's what Bebe always said.

BOYD: That bimbo second wife of yours. You probably couldn't even get it up for her in your old, dilapidated state. *(Silence.)* What? You couldn't?

WALTER: I'm not saying this exchange isn't going to have some advantages, Boyd.

BOYD: You couldn't get it up? Ha! Big, tough-talking tycoon and he can't get it up!

WALTER: It only happened once in a while. Natural. Happens to everyone.

BOYD: It's never happened to me.

WALTER: Is that the truth?

BOYD: Yes.

WALTER: Good. Let's give the old cooter a dry run, shall we? *(Walter starts rubbing his crotch.)*

BOYD: Get your hands off it, it's mine!

WALTER: Oooh weee! Why don't I call Bebe right now, I'm getting excited just thinking about her.
(Walter dashes to the phone and picks it up. Boyd slams it back down.)

BOYD: How could you have married her? She's half your age.
(Walter picks up the phone.)

WALTER: Not anymore she's not.

(Boyd slams the phone.)

BOYD: How could you do this to Mom?

(Walter picks up the phone.)

WALTER: Get over it! I divorced her ten years ago.

BOYD: You're going to meet up with Bebe?

WALTER: Yes. *(Walter starts dialing. Boyd's sudden lack of resistance registers with him. He hangs up.)* You don't think you're going to piggyback in on my action, do ya?

BOYD: Hey, it's my body.

WALTER: All this carping about her being a bimbo and you wanna get in her pants too?

BOYD: I was doing you a favor by going along.

WALTER: Forget it! I'm not meeting up with Bebe until we get this thing settled. Enough going around in circles. Let's have this out like men.

BOYD: What do you suggest?

WALTER: How about this: whoever admits they want to be like the other guy has to leave our body.

BOYD: It's not our body, it's mine. Besides, that's ridiculous. Who's going to admit that?

WALTER: It's fair. Fair all around. If you admit that you want to be like me you'll get your wish. And I'll get my wish. We'll both be happy. And if I admit that I want to be like you—well, I will deserve to die.

BOYD: I'm not going to admit I want to be like you because I don't. All my life I've been running away from your godawful example.

WALTER: So you got nothing to worry about. Shall we call it an agreement?

BOYD: Get lost. I'm not cutting any deals with you.

WALTER: Whatsa matter? You scared?

BOYD: Leave me alone.

WALTER: If you really don't want to be like me you got nothing to lose. Unless of course…you're keeping a little secret. Huh?

BOYD: Leave me alone.

WALTER: Do you secretly want to be like Daddy?

BOYD: Get off my back.

WALTER: Agree then.

BOYD: Why?

WALTER: Agree! You got nothing to lose or something to hide.

BOYD: All right! All right, already.

WALTER: As the Devil is our witness?

BOYD: As the Devil is our witness.

(They shake on it.)

WALTER: That's good, Boyd. Let's talk now.

BOYD: We have been talking.

WALTER: If you don't want to be like me why do you want what I have? Why do you kill me for my money? Why do you wanna screw my wife?

BOYD: That's great, Dad. That really sums you up. You are what you own, right? The money in the bank. The stocks and bonds. The trophy wife. Man, you are deep.

WALTER: You're just like me, Boyd. You value the same things. Why do you think you killed me?

BOYD: No. We're night and day, Dad.

WALTER: The only difference is I earned it. You want to score it

BOYD: It's not the money, it's how you spend it. I wouldn't have cheated Mom out of a decent settlement, for instance.

WALTER: Give me a break. She made out like a bandit.

BOYD: I'm not getting into this.

WALTER: Good. Look: forget about the money for a second. Look into your heart. What do you see? Envy. You envy the force of my personality. You have all your life. I've seen it in your eyes—ever since you were yeay-high. 'Fess up, Boyd. You want to be like me, don'tcha?

BOYD: Dad: let me be clear about this. So you understand. So we don't have to keep playing this stupid game. I think you've really messed up your life bad. You gave nothing back to the people that loved you and that is the worst thing that can be said about a man. I don't want to be like you.

(Silence.)

WALTER: You feel that strongly about it, huh?

BOYD: Yes. I do.

WALTER: Well, I'm dead now. You killed me. I guess that'll serve me right.

BOYD: That's just it, Dad. You're not even dying in a considerate way.

WALTER: I should just fade away then. Is that it?

BOYD: Well, yes. Please?

WALTER: Maybe I should go then. But I want you to know, son. I wasn't as bad a father as you make out. Remember the time you got busted for selling drugs in college?

BOYD: It was just grass, Dad.

WALTER: My lawyers fixed it all up. I talked with the Dean—he got you reinstated in school. I fixed it all up. Does that sound like a bad dad?

BOYD: I was striking out on my own. I didn't need you there to remind me that I'd failed.

WALTER: How about the time you hit that game-winning run in the little league championship game? Do you remember that?

BOYD: How could I forget. All the guys on my team carrying me on their shoulders. Amazing.

WALTER: I bought the kids in the other team off.

BOYD: *You what?*

WALTER: How do you think you got such a fat pitch?

BOYD: I thought you were going to say how proud you were of me. You tell me you bought them off?

WALTER: What harm was there in that? You didn't find out about it, did you?

BOYD: Until now!

WALTER: I'm just telling you because…

BOYD: Dad, this is a memory that I've cherished all my life, *and you've just spoiled it!*

WALTER: I'm just telling you this because I want you to know how much I…how much I love you, son.

BOYD: That's not what you do when you love a kid. If you love him, you let him do it himself.

WALTER: The kid threw flames…

BOYD: I don't care! I don't care! I would rather have struck out than be the hero in those circumstances.

WALTER: Well...

BOYD: You see, Dad, that's our relationship in a nutshell. That is everything that is wrong with us.

WALTER: I'm sorry.

BOYD: You're sorry?!

WALTER: I'm just saying this to reach out.

BOYD: Reach out?

WALTER: There's something else. You might think I'm upset about your killing me.

BOYD: You're not upset that I killed you?

WALTER: Well, Boyd. There's something my father used to say. He'd say: In this world, son, there are two types of people. There's the takers...and there's the crumb-collectors.

BOYD: You've told me that a thousand times.

WALTER: Wisdom. Passed from father to son. Through the generations.

BOYD: And you always finished off by saying: "Son—you'll always be a crumb-collector."

WALTER: Did I say that?

BOYD: Yes! You did.

WALTER: Well, my point is...you've finally become a taker.

BOYD: I have?

WALTER: Yes. When you killed me. I know. Ironic, isn't it? But you saw what you wanted...and you took it. Good for you.

BOYD: You're not mad at me?

WALTER: Well...let's just say I have some pleasantly mixed feelings about it.

BOYD: That's incredible, Dad, because...when I was planning on doing this I kept thinking—well, I thought it was just justifying myself but I thought—this is exactly what Dad would do in these circumstances.

WALTER: And you might be right, son.

BOYD: Yes.

WALTER: And why was that important to you?

BOYD: Well, because...You bastard.

WALTER: You thought it. Say it.

BOYD: No.

WALTER: You killed me because you wanted to be like me. 'Cause its what I would have done. Say it.

BOYD: You tricked me. You tricked me!

WALTER: Only to show you to yourself, son. You can lie to me but you can't lie to yourself.

BOYD: No!

WALTER: Say it. I'm stronger than you. We can't live together here forever.

BOYD: No!

WALTER: Say it. It's the easiest way, son. Say it.

BOYD: Please...

WALTER: There's no way out. Say it.

BOYD: *I want to be like you!!!*

(Boyd falls on his back, apparently dead. Walter picks himself up. He walks to the phone.)

WALTER: Hello, Bebe? You won't believe what just happened.

(The light snaps to black.)

Family Of Horrors

William Gadea

Scene: here and now

Serio-comic
Biff: a well-meaning brother, 30s

Here, Biff explains how his brother, Ray, came to lose his head.

BIFF: *(As himself.)* Hold it there, Lorraine! I think I can answer that question. *(Ray rolls his eyes and crosses his arms disgustedly. As Biff drifts into the reverie of memory a light isolates him; the sounds of the scene he describes can be heard.)* Many years ago Ray and me were two perfectly normal kids growing up in the American heartland. Every morning before school our Mama would kiss us goodbye, and every morning she'd say to me: "Look after your brother, Biff. Now that your Dad is gone you have to look out for him." Porky was the bully of my grade. One day at lunchtime he was pushing me around like usual…when a ball came bouncing between us. And who should come running after it? My little brother Ray. Laughing, Porky and his friends grabbed Ray and carried him away. I tried to get them to stop but…there were too many of them. Before I knew it they were screwing him head first into a drain-hole behind the gym. I yelled "stop, stop!" but they wouldn't stop. They wouldn't stop until his head was stuck in the drain-hole up to his shoulders. I was crying! I didn't know what to do. I should have called for help, but all I could think about was getting him out. I didn't know any better. I pulled him by his ankles! I pulled and pulled as hard as I could and then: I heard a pop. Like champagne being uncorked. And I heard his head…as it rolled down the drain. Down the drain…and out of our lives forever. It is true—I have failed Ray. There's nothing I can do to give him his head back. But I can try to make up for it! And I will! And—he always cries when I get to this part— *(Ray's shoulders are shaking, but only because he's laughing.)* I'm going to do everything in my power to give him a normal life. My little brother is going to have everything an ordinary guy would have—a place to live, hobbies, a TV—yes, even a girlfriend! That much I have promised him, and that much will I do for him. That's pretty much the long and the short of it.

Feasting

S. P. Miskowski

Scene: a field

Dramatic
Henry: A man haunted by his experiences in war, 20–30

> *Once a soldier, Henry now works as a surveyor. Here, he reveals a bit of his empty soul to Joseph, his partner.*

HENRY: But I don't. And here's what I keep thinking: how would I know anything else, if I don't know what it is I actually do for my wages? What good am I? *(Joseph stares at him, he goes on.)* All right. Nature.—For example.—What do I know about nature? I was a soldier. I've seen everything. Flood. Drought. Murder. Famine. Revolution. Four thousand soldiers drowning in a river, holding onto the reins of their horses and drowning. Two men killing each other—both dying—in the very ditch they're fighting over. Does any of this mean anything? Is it just the nature of the world? Or is God himself poking his head into the world to scare everybody? You see? *(Joseph shakes his head; no.)* I don't know anything. Do you? My whole life is used up with living. Some days, it's all I can do to wake up. There's putting on socks. Then there's putting on trousers. Then filling a sack with things like this— *(He holds up the dial again.)* You see what I'm saying? *(Joseph thinks about it, then shakes his head.)* I get worn out just thinking about the socks, boots, trousers, waking up and walking…When will it end? When I die, and some other stupid land surveyor has to get up, and put on his socks…

Fragments

John Jay Garrett

Scene: events during the life and death of Jack Wilson

Serio-comic
Jack: a young man on the verge of adulthood, 15

> *Jack's best friend has tricked him into asking out Rachel.*
> *Here, Jack makes an awkward attempt to convince her to go*
> *out on a date.*

JACK: I...um...so how are...what do you...hi. Oh God, this is so
stupid, look my name is Jack Wilson and I've been sent here to
ask you out.

[RACHEL: Really?]

JACK: Wait, don't say anything. Okay, look. I know this seems
queer, but...trust me, it isn't what it seems like.

[RACHEL: It isn't?]

JACK: Well maybe it is. I've got two friends standing right behind
you that you shouldn't look at... *(Rachel does and continues to
listen to him, indifferent.)* ...or maybe you should. Anyway we
have this dare thing where we each put in two dollars and we
rotate whose turn it is and whose turn it is to dare and if the person does it, he gets four dollars, and if he loses, he has to pay
four dollars. *(Jack, flustered, looks to his friends, who wave him
on violently, jumping in the air.)* I know it's extremely childish, and
may not appear to be much fun, but when you get to dare someone, it can actually be quite, ah...stimulating. You know, trying
to concoct something truly devious, which I did and ah...you're
my punishment.

[RACHEL: I'm your punishment, huh?]

JACK: I mean, God that sounds really bad. God, I'm saying God a
lot. *(Sighs.)* Only punishment in the sense that this is excruciating
for me, because I have no luck with girls and my palms go all

36

sweaty and my mind goes everywhere else. And Doug just picked you seemingly at random, but I know he knows that I've been looking over at you for the past fifteen minutes because I think you're really...beautiful. God, that sounds cheesy. Doug just knows, he just knows when I really like someone, and he thinks it's so much fun to torment me. And I don't know why I like you so much, maybe because you were talking to yourself over here and I just find that very engaging and really...cute. I don't know. *(Again Jack looks to Michael and Doug. The two jump around and start making all kinds of crazy faces, trying to throw him off. Jack takes a deep breath and slows down.)* Look, if you say yes, we get four dollars to go on a date to Heids and that wouldn't be all bad, would it? I mean, when I'm not rambling, I can be sort of funny. Actually, when I am rambling I can be sort of funny too. Hey, it's summer in Syracuse, something this place sees very rarely, the lake's gorgeous, and we could just get some hot-dogs and walk on the parkway and I don't know, talk about little things I guess, and I can think about how much fun it is to be with you, and maybe you'd think the same thing about me.

Fragments

John Jay Garrett

Scene: events during the life and death of Jack Wilson

Dramatic
Ethan: a young man struggling to know his dead father, 18

> *Ethan's father, Jack, died in Vietnam before he was born. Here, Ethan visits the Vietnam War Memorial in Washington, DC and reads a letter that Jack wrote when he found out that he was going to be a father.*

ETHAN: So there you are. Jack Wilson. My father. I don't know if I should be here. I don't have any memories of you. All I have is this hole inside me. Sometimes I wish I could have never been born and you could still be alive, then all this pain your death brought to the world wouldn't be here. Sometimes I hate you. How can I feel so empty when I see your name on this wall? God, there's so many of you. I told Grandma last week that I didn't want to come here and she gave me this. *(He unfolds the letter.)* I don't know if she was annoying while you were alive, but sometimes she can be a real pain in the ass. She said I should read it out loud here. She says that it gives her some kind of…well I'll just… *(He looks at the letter.)* Dear Mom. If I can ever say that I had a wonderful day in Vietnam, I know today will be the one I remember. Don't get me wrong, there was still lots of rain and mud and walking. But when we made camp and the choppers came, I sat down with a beer and a small stack of letters. I guess everyone wrote me at once. I read your letter and Aunt Joanne's and even one that Mr. Canty had sent me. I was already feeling pretty loved and a little less lonely when I read the last letter (Yes Mom, I save Rachel's letters for the end, but that doesn't mean I love you any less). I get tingles when I think about what she told me. I'm going to be a dad. Now I know you'll be mad and it might seem like this is bad news. But you're not over here. As I read her words it was like I was holding and smelling the baby right in my arms. I can not wait to see him. I know it's wrong to assume it will be a boy, but a daughter would be just as amazing. I'm gonna have a baby Mom. Can you believe that? Remember how I always said that the most important thing to me was one day having a family? Well now it's really coming true. Vietnam or not I think today is the happiest day I have ever seen. I don't know what else to say 'grandma.' I'm just gonna send this off and write you again when I'm not so overwhelmed. I love all of you. Jack. *(Ethan looks up from the letter.)* I'm trying to see this all rationally. You and I were never alive at the same time. Why do I feel like I talk to you every day? I do things sometimes, you know. I say something, or I laugh a certain way, and I just know that it's the you in me. I don't understand how you could die before I was even born, and yet...I can love you so much. It's stupid. I feel so stupid for loving someone I've never met. But in any of this, that is the only thing I'm sure of. I love you. I love you so much. My father. Jack Wilson. *(Ethan reaches out slowly, hesitantly, withdrawing several times. All sound has dissipated. He finally reaches out that little bit more...and touches his fathers name.)* Dad.

Gangster Apparel

Richard Vetere

Scene: Rikers Island

Serio-comic
Louis: a hitman contemplating entering the Witness Protection Program, 20–30

> *Patrician Louis is determined to get out of serving time as he here explains to Joey, his partner in crime.*

LOUIE: I don't want how to learn how to make it inside! Do you know why? Because I'm learnin' somethin' here on my own!

[JOEY: What are you learnin'?]

LOUIE: Did you see before? Did you see what happened here? How that mole from below the ground, that rat bastard who is nobody and knows nobody, gave me a look! He gave me a face! Me! Do you know why? Because Louie Falco don't mean nothin' in here! Louie Falco ain't nobody inside! Louie Falco is out there, on the street in the right restaurants and the right social club, and standin' on the right corner! That's what I'm learning here! I'm learnin' that if I stay here I'll have to be somebody else for the rest of my life! I can't be Louie Falco anymore! Joey, when I was a kid my father used to tell me this story about Al Capone. It seems that the Feds got Capone for cheatin' on his taxes. They put him away for ten years and when he was in prison the other inmates used to make fun of him. Do you know why? Because the guards had him washin' the floors, Joey! They had him washin' the floors with a bucket and a mop! Al Capone!

[JOEY: Wow…]

(Louie inches toward Joey.)

LOUIE: Joey, listen to me. In about ten minutes they are going to come for us, they are going to take us crosstown to court and our trial is going to start. Now, before that happens, I want you to think about somethin' I think we should take the D.A. up on her offer. *(Whispers.)* Witness protection.

Gangster Apparel

Richard Vetere

Scene: Arizona

Serio-comic
Louis: a hitman contemplating entering the Witness Protection
Program, 20–30

> *When Louis and Joey are relocated to Arizona by the Feds,*
> *Louis chafes at life in the desert. Joey, on the other hand,*
> *seems to finally come into his own. When he proudly shows*
> *Louis his garden, the former hitman is reminded of his father,*
> *a bricklayer.*

LOUIE: You got all this to grow out here? In the heat?

[JOEY: I got a green thumb, Louie.]

LOUIE: You know, my old man was like you. Except it wasn't flowers, it was *bricks.* Oh man, did he like to make things with bricks.
He made stoops, stairs, walls, you name it, if it had a brick in it,
he'd make it. I can see him right now like it was just yesterday, on
his hands and knees on the sidewalk with the mortar and the wet
rag, proud as a peacock, working till the sun went down. He left
his mark all over the neighborhood.

[JOEY: I remember seeing him doing that. How come you
never took after him?]

LOUIE: Me? Gettin' dirty? Get out of here. Sure, he tried to get me
interested. But come on. I still cringe thinkin' of gettin' that
cement stuck in my fingernails...But now, mother's brother, my
uncle Funzi? That man dressed like a king. He treated himself like
he was born to royalty. The best clothes, the best women, the
best cars. He could charm the dead. When I was a kid, I used to
look in the mirror and try to move like him, talk like him, act like
him.

[JOEY: Where is he now?]

LOUIE: Calvary cemetery. He died on my sixteenth birthday. My mother told me that he died in a car crash but how many people do you know who die in car crashes are found in the *trunk* of the car with twenty-seven bullet holes in 'em? *(Pause.)* Uncle Funzi, I wish he was alive today.

The Good Luck Charm

James M. O'Donoghue

Scene: NYC

Dramatic
Man: a petty thief-turned-killer, 20–30

Here, a killer weaves a gritty tale of betrayal and retribution.

MAN: See this? It's a Rabbit's Foot. Like you didn't know, right? What you probably don't know is that this one really works. I can remember exactly when I got it. Bought it from a candle/incense stand on 3rd Avenue. It was the night my luck began. It was a cold night last December and I was with my sometimes partner in crime Ronnie Stoops. Ronnie was a cross-dresser and street hustler. He loved going into supermarkets and copping an inhalant high from the Reddi-Whip. It helped him see his dreams of being a crime lord someday. Right. Anyway we had scoped out this garage in one of the big housing projects in the city. Little risk and we figured the attendant to have $400 maybe $500 in the till. No masks, we just pull our hats low, coat collars up and bull our way into the office. Spanish guy watching TV. Empty cans of Schaeffer beer in the trash. Falls out of his chair and onto the floor as we enter. Ronnie pushes a .45 into his face, screaming at him not to make a move. Like he was going somewhere, right. I head for the till, hit a No Sale and the drawer flies open. I'm looking at maybe eighty bucks. I yell to Ronnie that there is only punk change in the drawer. He grabs the attendant by the face bringing him to his feet. "Where the hell is the money!!?! Where the hell is the money?!!?" The guy is terrified. He points to the desk drawer, "It's all in there," he croaks. I yank the drawer and there's a bank bag. Opening it I see a couple of grand, easy. I turn to Ronnie, "Big time, man. Let's go!" Then all of a sudden Ronnie's face turns weird. He pushes the Spanish guy to the ground, putting the .45 to his head he says to me, "Why did you say my name? Now we are going to have to waste this guy. He knows my name!!" I have no idea what he is talking about. "I didn't say anybodys' name. C'mon let's get out of here." Ronnie sez that's no good. "You called me Marty. Now he knows my name is Marty!" I don't know what to think now. I don't know who the hell Marty is and I wish to God I didn't know who the hell Ronnie was. The poor Spanish guy is praying up a storm. I'm afraid that Ronnie is finally flipping out from his inhalant habit. I grab him by the sleeve and pull him towards the door. "Let the dude go. He told us where the cash was. He ain't telling nobody nothin'. Leave him, man." Ronnie turns and stares at the guy as if debating this when I pull him again and push him thru the door. I look at the guy on the floor and say, "Don't worry, man. Nobody is going to hurt you." I keep pushing Ronnie. Up the stairs and out into the street. Down the block, into the subway. Up to my place. Lock the door. Get some beers from the fridge. "What the hell was all that 'Marty' stuff about?? Have you lost your mind!! What were you gonna do, kill the guy??!" Ronnie with a big stupid smile on his face. "That 'Marty' stuff was my idea. When the cops come this guy is gonna tell them that he knows one of the guys names was Marty and so they go off spinning their wheels looking for some loser named Marty and the heat is off us." Ronnie sits back like he just discovered fire or something. I tell him that it's over for us two as a team. That he scared the hell out of me back there and was acting more and more irrational. His brain was being fried with chemicals. He gets up from the couch and demands his half of the money right now. No problem. I cut it up, $2700 apiece. Amazing. They must have been getting ready for a bank drop. Ronnie takes his share and walks out the door. Sez nothin'. Just as well. This guy was a major psycho just about to explode. Way too dangerous. I go to sleep. Party tomorrow, enough for one day. Next afternoon I'm parked in my favorite booth in my favorite bar, Billy's. No B.S. Just beer, booze, broads. They also sell smokes and Slim Jims. That's all you really need if you think about it. Couple of hours later the door opens and in pours this knock-out blonde in red leather pants. Sits at the bar. Being devoured by a hundred hungry eyes. Didn't seem to bother her one bit. Being on a roll I push once more and have a drink sent over to her. She picks up the shot and saunters over to my booth. I gesture for her to sit, real nonchalantly, like something this good happens to me all the time. Soon it's like we were old high school sweeties or something. Roll again, I figure, and ask her up to my place. Sounds great she says. Really? She walks all around my pad while I try to find some decent music to put on and a couple of clean glasses for the champagne we picked up on the way over. Taking off my coat she sees the .45 I hang under my arm. All excited. I try to just put it away but she insists on seeing it. Please take all the bullets out first though, she says. So I do. Throw the bullets onto the table and hand her the gun. She looks it over, tosses it on the couch. Pulls a silver plated .38 out of her pocketbook and points it at my head. I'm so wasted at this point that I have to close one eye to be sure of what' s going on. She tells me to sit in the chair and then ties my hands behind me with an extension cord. She apologizes for the cord and says she forgot to bring a silk scarf. Wants to know where I keep my money. I tell her where I would like to keep my foot and she lets me have a slap across the forehead with the .38. Major pain. She tosses the place and soon finds the stash in a hallowed-out book. Laughs at my imagination. Says I'm a real Sherlock. I tell her what she is and I get another hit in the head. She says she is sorry she can't stay but has a train to catch. Again with the apologies. She's gone. Takes me about fifteen minutes to get free and the rest of that night for my head to stop throbbing. All told I lost about $3400 and a lot of pride. Next day. I'm down on 14th street trying to scare up some cash and who do I see floating down the block but the nice lady in the red leather pants. Must have been a local train she had to catch. I follow carefully but she ain't even thinking that way. Real easy. And what do you know, she turns down 18th street and walks into Ronnie the maniac's building. O yeah. I give her five minutes to get herself settled in Ronnie's pad and then with my .45 in hand I come thru the door. From the look on their faces

I can tell I'm unexpected. A faux pas. Ronnie starts to say something but I cut him short with a backhand. This makes her nervous as hell. Ronnie made her do it. It's all Ronnie's fault you see.
Right, just don't try for your handbag, honey. I get some rope and
tell her to tie up Ronnie. Nice and tight. She's crying now. Ronnie
is screaming and cursing. He's gonna kill all of us when he gets
free. See how stupid this guy is? Now I tie her up with some rope,
mentioning how I am so sorry for not bringing silk or some such.
Where's the loot, luv? In the handbag and Ronnie's is under his
mattress. Like that's a better spot than my book? I got almost
eight grand now. A regular Rockerfeller. By this time Ronnie has
almost run out of all the standard curses and is having to make
up some new strings of words. Interesting but I did have to go.
She was still babbling and begging me to take her with me. She
doesn't want to be left alone with Ronnie. It turns out that she
loves me you see. My, my. Don't you worry about Ronnie, my
dear, he was just leaving anyways. I place the .45 against his head
and another eye appears over his nose. She tries pushing herself
away. Falls over backwards. I help her up. I tell her that I'm too
much of a gentleman to leave her here alone so I'm sending her
on ahead with Ronnie. As she figures this out, you're a real
Sherlock yourself I tell her, eyes growing wide I preempt a scream
by putting one into her throat. That's the big problem with beautiful dames. Where to shoot them so that you're not ruining
something, you know. Leaving the scene of the crime I walk
down the block and onto a bus. I stop at my Aunt's place and
hide my piece and most of the cash there. My Aunt fades in and
out of reality all the time which makes for a great safe house.
Then home again, home again, jigity jig. Two days after this the
cops arrive at my apartment for a few questions and a little line-
up. Seems that the Spanish guy from the garage recognized
Ronnie's picture from a newspaper story about the double homi-
cide. Apparently Ronnie and a young lady were executed by some
drug lords they had tried to double-cross. The papers had this
info from well placed sources. The cops had me on file as a asso-
ciate of Ronnie's so they wanted to show my puss to the atten-

dant. We get downtown and I figure that I'm done for. If he made Ronnie from a newspaper photo, he'll make me for sure. The Spanish guy gets up from a desk as I walk in, comes right up to me. There's a good several beats as he just looks at me. And I'll swear that I saw a slight grin in his eyes before he turns to the cops and says, "No, wrong guy. The guy who saved my life was a bit taller." He looks back to me but the cops are already turning me out the door, like I'm diseased. I don't pretend to know how this thing works. Or what happened to the rabbit that used to wear it but I do know that wherever I go this guy is coming with me.

The Handyman

Ronald Harwood

Scene: the Sussex countryside, England

Dramatic
Roman Kozachenko: a Ukranian citizen of the UK accused of war crimes, 78

> *Due to a change in British law, individuals suspected of having committed war crimes may now be formally charged. One such person is Roman, a seventy-eight year-old man accused of participating in the murder of 817 Jews in Ukraine. Here, the nearly senile Roman explains why he could never have killed in cold blood.*

ROMAN: Okay. I tell you. I hate Communists. Many Jews Communists. Many Jews NKVD, secret police, Stalin people all Jews. Jews have best jobs, in offices always, nice, clean jobs, because, you understand, Jews look after their own. Okay. I say you now, I not like Communists, I not like Jews. To me, the same. But, does not mean I kill Jews, does not mean I am murderer. No. You ask, I tell.

[MARIAN: And now?]

ROMAN: Now? We are not in Ukraine. I am not that man. I am not that Ukrainian. Okay, I speak bad English, funny accent, Major Leonard he say me, 'Romka, you speak Mau-Mau.' But now, I am British subject. I am different man.

[MARIAN: And you are saying that you took no part in any action involving the murder of Jews in 1941?]

ROMAN: Never, never, never. I went to priest. Village priest. I remember him like yesterday. Father Alexei. I ask him, please Father, what to do? Evil, I say him, evil is in our land, our village, everywhere, evil. You can smell, you can taste, like sulfur, you know the smell sulfur? You taste and smell sulfur day, night, in

the nose, in the mouth. Your eyes water with sulfur. This is .
it is like to live then, to live there. I say him, Father Alexei, I a .
Christian, I say him I cannot live here with these things, with this
sulfur, with this terrible evil. I must go. Where, he ask? Where you
go? Father Alexei, you understand, he ask where I will go? What
answer? No answer. Where I can go? War everywhere. Germans,
Russians, Poles, everywhere. War. He say me, Romka, we are all
damned. You understand? Damned. This from priest. We are all
damned. I remember. I cannot take breath. I have shock like light-
ning is to strike me. All damned. I remember also tears, tears from
that priest, good man, Father Alexei, tears run down cheeks.
Because, he say me, we are caught in Devil's trap, Romka. He
shout loud, damned. I not understand then. But now, now, I
understand.

Anniversary, Punk!

, Jr.

now

Dramatic

Al Bean-Fletcher: a man seeking justice for his son's murder. 45

> *On the first anniversary of his son's murder by a street punk,*
> *who has been freed after serving only nine months in a juve-*
> *nile detention center, Al prepares to exact vengeance of a*
> *more permanent nature.*

AL: Damn! One hundred-fourteen million, eight hundred-forty thousand seconds. One million, nine hundred-fourteen thousand minutes. Twenty-one thousand, nine hundred hours. Three hundred sixty-five days. Fifty-two weeks. Twelve months. I can't believe it s been a year. *(Beat.)* I remember it like it was yesterday. I was at the post office, preparing for my annual review. The phone rings. I assume it's my wife, calling to find out if I got promoted. I'm right. It's her. *(Beat.)* Our son had been shot on his way home from school. She was at the hospital. By the time I got there he was gone. *(Beat.)* Randall. Randall Bean-Fletcher. I wanted to name him Al after me. But making a boy go through life being called by another man's name just didn't seem right to me. Sure I had to do it. But I didn't have a choice. What can a newborn say when his daddy names him "Junior?" "Feed me!" That's about it. So when I became a daddy I decided to play God and change the rules. *(Beat.)* Most fathers would spend a day like this at the cemetery or picketing in front of the courthouse, demanding a retrial. My wife's at the cemetery right now with her mother. Not me. Cemeteries are like all other rituals of death— they're for the living. The dead don't care. Hell, they're dead. Besides, I'm tired of crying. Nope. Ain't gonna be no more tears coming out of these eyes. No, sir! I'm a man, goddamnit! Leave the whimpering and whining to the women and children. Real men don't cry—they get even. *(Beat.)* The kid who killed Randall was a year younger than him. Only fifteen years old. They caught him, locked him up for nine months, then let him out. Said he was no longer a "danger to society. Said he was "reformed." Sometimes, when I'm watering the lawn, I see him drive by my house in his mama's Honda, seat cocked back pimp-daddy style, lookin' like Snoop Hot Diggity Damn Dog. He don't say nothin', but I can hear him loud and clear: "I'm *free!* I'm *free!* And ain't nothin' you can do to *me,* old *dude.* Be *cool. (Beat.)* Kids can be so stupid. They think just because you're grown you gotta be responsible all the time, do the right thing; that you can't just nut up and go crazy, like them. Well, today, I'm pleading "temporary insanity."

Have It All

Robert Coles

Scene: here and now

Serio-comic
Chad: a gay man recalling a one-night stand, 30s

> *Here, Chad reminisces about the heyday of gay dance clubs like the Saint, and one night in particular.*

CHAD: It was a pre-Saint party. You know, a *pre-Saint party.* It was the third one of the evening. You know—the first one would just be you and your bestest best friends where you'd decide what to *wear.* And we'd *always* be late for the second party. Well, it wasn't my fault! I had my wardrobe planned *days* in advance. But *certain people* simply *couldn't* make up their minds. So we'd get to the *second* pre-Saint party with just *barely* enough time to do our drugs. *(He reacts as if some people in the audience were shocked at that.)* Well, *that's* what the *second* party was *for.* So then, you'd go to the *third* pre-Saint party, and by this time there were *scads* of people you *barely* knew coming from *their* second pre-Saint parties and they were dragging along *other* scads of people you didn't know at *all.* And Raymond—he was one of the scads. And he was not bad looking. A little older than I'd like, but *very* charming. I remember I was fixing myself a drink and he came up behind me and said, "I bet you're looking for the tonic." Just like that: "I bet you're looking for the tonic." And I said, "I *certainly* am." And he put a splash in my glass without our eyes ever leaving one another's. And, you know, my drugs were just beginning to hit and I said to myself, "This is the most handsome man I've ever seen in my life." By the time we got to the Saint, I had the house in Greenwich picked out—four-bedroom colonial on a cul-de-sac—and had moved on to deciding whether we'd honeymoon in Mykonos or Ibiza. I tore my shirt off the instant I got inside—well, I *always* did that—and we ran upstairs and danced and danced. I don't ever remember stopping. Except that I know that we made to the balcony eventually, and his tongue was down my throat…and I don't know *what* else… *(He takes a moment and remembers wistfully.)* And then we were back on the dance floor and the star machine was doing *incredible* things and we were *all* just looking up at the dome and ooh-ing and aah-ing and I felt like I was floating though heaven. *(Pause. He remembers how wonderful it was, then comes back to earth.)* But around nine or ten in the morning the ecstasy wore off. And Raymond—was that his name?—he didn't look so good any more. And he was droning on and on about…I don't know—was it opera? Blecch, opera. And I was suddenly very, *very* tired. "I'm sorry, you know, I really just have trouble sleeping if I'm not in my own bed," I said as I left, "but call me during the week and maybe we can get together and blah blah blah." And I saw him again, but only at the pre-Saint parties. The *third* ones, where there were scads of people and I could pretend to be very involved in a conversation with someone else. I would wave to him from across the room in a manner that would say, "Oh, hi! I see it's you over there, and I'm smiling and being friendly and polite, but you're supposed to *know* that I *don't* want you to come over and bother me." And he didn't. But to be safe, I made sure that I *didn't* fix myself a drink.

Hawk Dreaming

Frank Cossa

Scene: a southern college town

Serio-comic
Joe: a filmmaker, 40

> *When a friend despairs of ever being able to understand women, Joe offers the following helpful information.*

JOE: Okay, let me explain it to you. First they have to go to the bathroom. Then it's too cold. Then they're concerned. Then they're hungry. Then it's their period. Then you forgot their birthday. Then they say "All you think about is sex." Then they're deeply moved. Then they're not speaking to each other. Then it's too hot. Then they ate too much. Then they can't deal with it. Then they can't stand their hair. Then they have to go to the bathroom again. Then they say "We never make love anymore." Then they're on a diet. Then they can't sleep. Then their feelings are hurt. Then they should've brought a sweater. Then they love each other. Then they hate their haircut. Then they can't walk in these shoes. Then it's their period again. And they have to go the bathroom.
   [GEORGE: That's it?]
JOE: That's it. Then you die of old age.

How To Go Out On A Date In Queens

Richard Vetere

Scene: a bar in Queens

Dramatic
Artie: a man suffering through a horrible date, 30s

> *Artie has mistakenly agreed to go out on a date with Laura,*
> *a loquacious and shallow woman with several ex-husbands*
> *to carp about. Here, beleaguered Artie finally explains why*
> *he wants to end the date and go home.*

ARTIE: Okay. I've been sitting here watching everyone and I know I don't fit in. It's like the cars I fix. I fix some big shot's car but I have nothing in common with him. He owns the car but I know it better than he ever will. And maybe that's how people are? They don't want to really know anything really about anyone else. That takes too much out of them. Well, Amy, you are a nice girl and you try and say the right thing but you are too nice to be dating my pal, Stan. Stan is a professional dating machine. He goes on what, 3.5 dates in a week? And what percentage of those dates are fun, Stan? Fifty five percent? He knows more about dating than anybody should know. He alone keeps all the restaurants and bowling alley's in Queens alive! But he's what? Thirty five and he still lives with his mother? *(To Stan.)* Why not fall in love and get married? You know why? Because dating is a recreation without anything serious to it. Sure, he keeps an apartment but isn't he over there every night he is not on a date?

[STAN: Hey, pal, let's talk about this at work Monday, huh?]
ARTIE: And Laura, you are a nice lady but you said you want to get to know me? I doubt it. I am in trouble, Laura. Big trouble. Because, for the first time in my life, I am alone. This is the first time I have been on a date since I was seventeen. On that first

date I fell in love with a woman who became my wife: Debbie. She lived down the block from me and we knew each other since the first grade. Yeah, we got married and right after we graduated and bought a house and planned on having kids but she didn't want them right away and neither did I. Well then there were money worries and other things but we stuck it out and tried but she couldn't get pregnant. We went to doctors to check the both of us out and there wasn't any problem. So, we figured, hell, if it happens, it happens. Anyway, guess what? We didn't need anyone else. We spent every night together and every weekend locked in the house having wonderful sex and sleeping and eating and just being. Know what I mean? But then, one day, one lousy rainy day, a truck's brakes locked on the highway and he skidded off the road into Debbie's car. That was it. One bad break. One lousy afternoon and she was gone. Like that. Worse than anything I have ever felt. How awful.

[AMY: How awful.]

ARTIE: Well, that was three years ago and this is the first time I am talking to another woman sitting this close to me who's not a relative. You know why? Because I don't want to meet anyone else. I don't want to know anyone as well as Debbie. Because no one will know me as well as she did. So, I don't read any newspapers and I don't keep up with current events. I don't care what goes on in the world. Let it go to hell, for all I care. I am in mourning. Not for Debbie, she's gone. But for me. For myself. Because I miss her. I miss her worse than I miss anything I ever knew. I miss her voice, her face, her little feet, her bad jokes and in the middle of the night I miss her titties, yes, her titties, Stan. And I don't want to replace her. So, you want to know me, then know what I am feeling. I am feeling grief and loss and emptiness.

(Long pause.)

[LAURA: My God.]

[AMY: I didn't know.]

[STAN: This is not a very good date.]

Infrared

Mac Wellman

Scene: NYC and the infrared mirror world

Dramatic
Narrator: an ungainly self in search of validation, 30–40

> *The narrator is a being whose sole purpose seems to be that of proactive self-discovery. Following a rather surreal visit to the world of infrared, he muses on how much more he has to learn about life.*

NARRATOR: All this seems so strangely familiar to me. All this I know, as if by *deja vu,* from some other world linked to this one by Time's worm-hole, and there is so much I want to learn. So much to learn. Before…before they come for me, as I am certain they will. Because of the shadow, the shadow that was not mine, that I brought with me all the way from the world of Infrared… (In truth, the Shadow is acting like a bag full of schizophrenic alley cats. An ominous black sedan pulls up. The sedan is filled with dark red light. Two men dressed in black get out. They both carry blackjacks and are masked. Our Narrator doesn't see them, but his shadow does and quakes with fear.) I want to learn why a thing can resemble another thing, but not be at all the same; I want to know where our dreams come from, and how it is possible for us to desire things that injure us, or drive us mad; I want to know what the true limits of the human condition are—and how we are to know when we have gone too far—when we have disappeared into the hole of our own undoing; I want to know why I have become so disfigured that I cannot bear my own image, and even my own shadow is a visual horror to me; I want to know what love is, and why when you reach to hold it, it flies off in terror like the uncaged paroquet, confused by sudden freedom; I want so badly to know why oh why is there anything at all…

Jack And Jill

Jane Martin

Scene: here and now

Dramatic
Jack: a man whose marriage is in jeopardy, 30s

> *Jill's residency is proving more than their marriage can bear,
> and Jack can no longer provide her with the kind of support
> she needs to endure the long hours and stress. During a
> rather serious argument, Jill accuses Jack of being too
> involved with trying to be nice to be truly effective. Here, Jack
> fumes over being called "nice."*

JACK: Nice, right? Nice. Okay. One second. One second. This nice
we are talking about here…"don't be nice, Jack." This "nice" has
a bad name…to say the goddamn least. Women, to generalize,
hate nice…no, they like it in clerks, they like it in auto mechan-
ics…but…nice guys finish last, right? Why? Because "nice" is
essentially thought to lack complexity, mystery. "Nice" just…has
no sex appeal…it just doesn't understand the situation. Women
distrust "nice" because, given the cultural context, they themselves can't possibly be nice. How can the powerless be "nice."
What good is nice to the "exploited?" So women loathe nice
because they see, they know what a phony mask it is in their own
lives, so when they perceive it in a man it just pisses them off.
What they prefer are abusive qualities moderated by charm,
because they are already abused personalities, given the culture.
I'm not kidding. Hey, I don't buy it because there is another
"nice," a hard-won, complex, covered-with-blood-and-gore
"nice." An existential, steel willed, utterly crucial and necessary
"nice" that says to the skags in the motorcycle gang, "Fuck you
and the hogs you rode in on. I exemplify hope and reason and
concern." See, I raise the fallen banner high, Jill, so satirize me,

shoot me, stab me, dismiss me, go screw the Four Horsemen of the Apocalypse if that's what turns you on, I'm nice!! *(He slowly turns into himself. Jill enters and sits by stack of books.)* Sorry, I didn't, uh...don't know how I got into that...just "nice," you know...well, anyway, sorry.

The John Doe Variations

Silas Jones

Scene: the empty front room of Yomoma's Rest Home

Serio-comic
Yomoma: an eccentric gay man, 50s

> *Here, the enigmatic Yomoma uses make-up and costumes to transform himself into "the kissing cousin of Aunt Jemima" as he explains why he decided to open up a rest home.*

YOMOMA: *(Sings.)* "Went to the doctor/the doctor said/Moma's little baby needs short'ning bread." *(Pause.)* Reality don't work for you no mo' neither, hunh? Oh come on, admit it, that's why yawl here. To see me perform. Cause everybody loves a stereotype. All you savage individualists out there, you know the piss-poor truth, don't you: Individuality only works in private. In public, it's a slave in drag, Slow Death in lipstick. Better wake up. Act real…embrace that dreadful facsimile on your drivers permit. Or walk. "Put on the skillet, neen-a-mind the lid, Moma's little baby needs short'ning bread. Moma's little baby loves short'ning, short'ning/Moma's little baby—" Ah, a stereotype's grace. "Amazing Grace/how sweet it sounds—" When I was young and pretty and shacked up with Immortality, I was an actor—type cast, of course. One night I looked into my dressing room mirror and Oh! Girl, you old, time to talk serious. A character actor you're not. What are you going to do when you retire? I happened to have my tv on. Remember Lon Chaney Jr. in that Wolfman flick? Remember the scene where the toothless old gypsy woman with a lisp is driving her creaky little one-horse cart through the woods when she hears this ungodly howl? The full moon's dying, the dawn is dawning, the Wolfman's changing back from Wolfman to man, right? Oh he's howling pitifully, fangs out, face all hairy, got these evil signs growing in his paws,

60

remember? And the saintly little gypsy cradles the Wolfman in her arms, makes the sign of the cross and whispers those immortal lines, "My son, you have been cursed. May God have mercy on your soul." That's what I'm gonna do when I retire, I said to myself, I'm gonna save the little wolfmen of the world. So noble the cause it brought tears to these old eyes. Did you know that every ten seconds a Wolfman is born? It's true. So, with my meager savings I bought this house and turned it into—da-daaaaah— Yomoma's Rest Home! Thus began my quest to return the little wolfmen of the world to a state of grace, the grace of a stereotype. Somewhere out there, at this very minute, the womb of Reality slips, and another Wolfman is born. If he ends up here, I *(Stands.)* Yomoma, will teach him a stereotype's grace. No autographs please… *(Howls.)*

King Gordogan

Radovan Ivsic
Translated by Roger Cardinal
American Version by Allan Graubard

Scene: the fantastical kingdom of King Gordogan

Serio-comic
Tinatine: the son of King Gordogan, 20s

> *Tinatine is in search of his true love, who has been impris-*
> *oned in a white tower. Here, the luckless young man com-*
> *plains about his fruitless search.*

TINATINE: Such a cruel fate. What have I come to? They say that
love brings happiness, that flowers sprout beneath the feet of
those in love. If that we're true, I'd be happy. There's not a single
mountain, not a single forest that my feet haven't crossed. The
entire kingdom should be covered in flowers. I've searched so
much that I've found the lair of the scarlet bear with green eyes,
even the lair of the green bear with scarlet eyes; but what I'm
really looking for slips through my fingers like the breeze. Why on
earth go on living? I'll never track the White Tower down. If I go
to the right, the Tower's on the left. If I go left, it turns up—on
the right. If I think it's in front of me, it's bound to be at my back.
I'm so exhausted I could weep. What should I do? And love! love!
All the misfortunes of the world pour on my head. I burn for
White. Yet she's never seen me, not once. And even if we met,
she'd hate me. I'm Gordogan's son, who stole her throne, who
locked her up in the White Tower and killed her father, the White
King; at least, that's what everyone says. I've looked for her everywhere, in every corner. No luck. When I think that wild beasts
might be tearing her to shreds, I can't bear the sadness! But that's
not the worst. Even if she were alive, and I did find her, even if
she liked me—can I hope for that?—there would still be my royal

father Gordogan. He'd frustrate us for sure. Such woe!...But what's this? The White Tower? It's the first time it's appeared by day. The vision comes only at night. All at once. Dazzling, looming up, the White Tower. You step, look carefully, it's not the White Tower, but White, smiling, holding out her arms. You run to her, it's a glow worm under a bush. It's no good, White, dart about all you want, I'm not fooled. I know you're not the White Tower. You may be a white ant, or a butterfly, but you're not the White Tower, however much your white skin shines! Tinatine, Tinatine, how sad you are. But, hey, Tower, why are you still there? I'll count to three. Be careful. You'll vanish! Do you hear? One, two, three. You don't want to move? OK, it's all right, I'll leave. You won't lead me about by the nose. For the last time: disappear! You're not the White Tower. Your tricks are useless. Go away! I'll count again: one, two—Tower, I've gotten to two, please go away. Three! Stubborn, huh? It won't work. You'll live to regret it. *Bon chance,* Tower, you'll never see me again. Tinatine, why should you leave, after all, this creature might just *be* the White Tower, the one you've been looking for in vain, through immense forests, on razor thin crags. The horror! No, no, Tinatine, you're dreaming. It would be better to go and wake up. I'm in a dream *(Pinches himself.)* Ouch! Ouch! I can't be dreaming, if I can see something that doesn't exist. The White Tower isn't here, yet I can see it. I must be dreaming, such a pleasant dream. No complaints now! I'll never wake up. *(Approaches tower.)* It's hard. I can't even break it with a stone. Look at this. *(Pounds stone on tower.)*

King Gordogan

Radovan Ivsic
Translated by Roger Cardinal
American Version by Allan Graubard

Scene: the fantastical kingdom of King Gordogan

Serio-comic
The Fool: the King's fool, 20–50

> *Here, the talkative Fool indulges in some rather philosophical stream of consciousness.*

FOOL: What the cradle has rocked, the spade dig's under. Ah yes, Fool, such is life. One day you're kicking and the next…the next, you're gone. An old wise man told me that. What did the old wise man tell you? Dust marches over dust. That's what he told me. I don't understand. But of course, it's very simple. You sprinkle water on an egg and there you are: *tsip, tsip, tsip,* an oak starts to sprout! Where does it come from? Straight up out of the dust. A storm knocks it over, and *tsip, tsip, tsip,* the oak's gone. Gone where? Into the dust. Do you think a goat's anything other than dust, just because it goes *mee? Mee*—and it's finished! No more, *mee*. The wind blows it all away. Life's not so polite. It jumps into a speck of dust, changes into a flower or a fish; and the speck of dust thinks: aye aye, I'm a flower; aye aye, I'm a fish. And then, life hops, jumps, runs off, picks up a new speck of dust, just when you expect it least. Naturally it won't stand still…naturally. It's as faithless as a waterfall. Fool, you've spoken some words of wisdom today.—I've spoken some words of wisdom today?—Yes. When a fool speaks words of wisdom, then…—What?—Do you know what?—No.—Then he's bound to die, that self-same day; that's what they say.—What are you trying to tell me? Poor Fool! Yes, yes, if I start saying words of wisdom, I'll die the self-same day. But why should I die today? It's

Tinatine who'll die today. Such a pretty gibbet for him, eh! Fine indeed. I should say so! Tinatine's going to dangle up there and wriggle about like a worm sliced in two. It's Tinatine who'll be hanged, not you. You hear someone say you're gonna be hanged, and then you imagine that someone is you! It's not the first time I've seen a gibbet.—Are you kidding?—No, I'm not.— Don't you believe these stupid ideas! Wait a minute! I see a way out! All I need to know is whether I've actually said anything at all!

The Lady With The Toy Dog

Sari Bodi

Based on the short story, *The Lady With the Toy Dog* by Anton Chekhov

Scene: a seaside resort in Yalta, the turn of the century

Serio-comic
Dimitri: a sophisticated cad, 30–40

> *Here, a man addicted to the joys of romantic pursuit makes a canny observation regarding his quarry.*

DIMITRI: One should always pay attention to the color of a woman's gloves. A woman wearing grey gloves is for certain an easy conquest. It signifies that she doesn't wish to be noticed. She would like to fade into the background. But with each word I speak to her, her sense of herself magnifies, and by the "Where do you come from?" she is mine. White gloves tell me the woman is fastidious, and would not be much fun frolicking in the bed sheets. Blue gloves, the color of sky, tells me she has an imagination and would amuse me for awhile, until I tired of her incessant imaginings of other women in my bed. Did you notice the color of Anna Sergeyenev's gloves? I will tell you. They are lilac colored. It is a young color, and it is a long time since I have been young.

Losers Of The Big Picture

Robert Vivian

Scene: a summer home

Dramatic
Rummy: prosperous but dismayed, 50s

> *Rummy stands on the threshold of his golden years with a nice pocketful of money but no understanding of life; past, present or future.*

RUMMY: My wife loves flowers more than people and my mistress—or excuse me, my *ex*-mistress—is going to marry Jack. I think congratulations are in order. Where's the champagne?

[JEAN: Out. We drank the last bottle this morning.]

RUMMY: *(Faces Jean.)* I don't know why I get drunk with you—maybe it's because you're my sister and I figure what the hell. No small thing in the pressure cooker we call a home. *(Pause. He fidgets slightly in his chair. Beryl enters in a bathrobe, arms crossed.)* Still, not too long ago I was a young man with big hopes and dreams and a beautiful, intelligent wife. How times change. Mind you, I'm not bitter or depressed. But somewhere I took a wrong turn and it has nothing to do with Ms. Love Button. I taste ashes in my mouth. I was sold a bill of goods and I swallowed the whole thing, part and parcel—career, family, and a way to clean my arteries. Who was I kidding? *(Anguished.)* I always wanted…to help people in some small way. You think I'm joking but I'm not. I'm dead serious. But…things have a way of getting out of hand. You lose focus, a sense of priorities. You go under and the rest of the world applauds your efforts because you have a Mercedes Benz and Haagen Dass in the freezer. Son-of-a-bitch. It's no way to spend your golden years.

Magnets
Phil Hines

Scene: Troy, NC

Serio-comic
Warren: a man who has just realized his marriage is over. 30s

> *When his wife's artistic slump is cured by the arrival of her old*
> *flame, Warren realizes that he can't compete with her pas-*
> *sion for art—nor does he wish to try. Here, he tells his wife*
> *and her suspected lover about a liberating experience he*
> *enjoyed at a dinner given in his honor by the Jaycees.*

WARREN: Now, Patsy, honey—if you want me to tell this—my little
story—you gonna have to hush a minute. I had a little bit to drink
tonight but not that much so I'm not fixin' to tell you a drunk
story—'cause you see I was sober. Dead sober almost. But I was
drinking. You know I was drinking. They had drinks there.

[PATSY: Yes.]

(During the following, Warren is up, moving about the room.
His movements are exaggerated. He finally has their atten-
tion and he becomes the wild stand-up comic—too proud to
show them the pain underneath. He is seemingly amused by
everything.)

WARREN: Well, your Young Man of the Year decided not to worry
about how many drinks I had 'cause I was so uh—proud. Proud
of winning such a magnificent award. Proud, you know what I
mean? So when it came time for my speech, I was—maybe a bit
tipsy—but I knew what I was doing. Just didn't know what it was
going to be till it was done, know what I mean?

[PATSY: Yes, Warren.]

WARREN: Anyway, Jefferson got up to introduce me. You know
Jefferson, Preacher?

[CAM: I don't think so.]

WARREN: Big shot. President of the Fidelity Bank. Anyway, he got up and he started talkin' 'bout the qualities they looked for in their Young Man of the Year. And there I was 'bout half looped—knowing that any minute he was gonna call my name and I was gonna strut up there and give my little speech and—damnit, I knew I couldn't do it. So when he got to the part about the future and how I was a—uh—representative of the new young progressive small businessman of the '90s, I started to crack up inside. You know why, Patsy? 'Cause that's what I been trying to be since the '80s and now that I'm almost it—I ain't gonna be it 'cause it stinks! It's nothing! The whole damn thing is nothing! I only thought it would be—something. The cream of the crop, he called me. It was scary. He was talking a damn foreign language—a language I always thought I wanted to talk. And he was talking about me! Talking in some secret code that, by God, I was beginning to understand. 'Bout how I was the foundation—the brick—for building a better America! Hell, I ain't no brick, I thought! And then…then he got to the part about how I was especially outstanding this year. Outstanding for what? What the hell am I outstanding for, I kept thinkin'. *(Moves to Patsy.)* Then it hit me—just as big and bright as that damn sun! Hit me so hard it bumed me through and through—! I am outstanding, damnit! 'Cause I'm not goin' up there and talk about how I believe all that crap—all that crap that's supposed to be make you "fulfilled" as he said. Proud. Happy. Hell, no! I'm gonna tell 'em all the truth, I decided. So I did. I did, Patsy. I walked up to that podium and looked out and stared at 'em for a long time. And I told them I only knew one thing—that I had decided what was wrong with the world. I told them that I only knew one thing to be true. *(Pause. He becomes very serious, intense.)* The big problem with all of us is—too—much—oatmeal.

[CAM: *(After a pause.)* What?]

WARREN: Too much oatmeal—and not enough bagels. *(Moving around the room, stops at Patsy, leans in to her.)* Gimme bagels. Or pancakes. But big pancakes! Thick pancakes. Or heroes. Gimme some heroes! Something with substance. For God's sake, gimme something with a little substance. *(Silence and then Patsy begins to laugh.)* And then I started laughing at 'em. Laughing like crazy. Laughed my ass off. Couldn't help it. They all looked at me. Waiting for somebody to come and take me out. But nobody could move. I just laughed my way right outta the room.

(Patsy is laughing to herself. Cam laughs slightly, confused. Warren sits, then puts his hands to his face, gets quiet. Cam rises, stops next to couch, watches Warren and Patsy.)

[PATSY: That must have felt kinda wonderful.]

WARREN: Yeah.

[PATSY: You'll blame me later—but that's ok.]

WARREN: Naw...'cause, you see, it don't matter.

[PATSY: I should have been there for you. You've always been there for me. It is my fault.]

WARREN: Naw, it's me. I just didn't know any better. You see, I've always asked for a little bit. And sometimes when you ask for a little bit, you get nothing, right, Preacher?

(Cam rises, looks toward kitchen.)

[CAM: Let me get your coffee.]

WARREN: Sit down. I don't want coffee. *(Cam sits.)* After my little speech, I didn't know what to do with myself. So I drove around for awhile. Got kinda sad. So I thought, what next? What would feel—right? So I went to my little shrine. My little Sweetheart Burgers. Named after Patsy. And I looked at it real good and I looked at me real good. Thought about my daddy. How he wanted me to stay on the farm. Wanted me to grow things. Be a dirt farmer. "Hell, no, Pop! I ain't gonna do that! I'm gonna be something big! I'm gonna marry Patsy Glover and I'll be the richest man in this damn town! I'm gonna work my balls off! Hell, I'm gonna do it for me—and for Patsy!" You know what really kills me, Preacher? Now everybody's talking 'bout the environment and talkin' bout finding a little farm, growing organic food and livin' off the land. Shit! Just when I learn the new, they come and change it back to the old. *(Moves center.)* So I stood there and I looked at that grill and I knew something was all screwed up in me, you know what I mean?—and it had something to do that place. And I decided I had to burn it down. I knew I'd be happy, real happy if—

[PATSY: Warren, no!]

WARREN: If I could just stand there and watch Sweetheart Burgers burn right down to a Crisp. That I could start over and—

[CAM: Warren! Do you realize the kind of trouble you'll be in when—]

WARREN: I didn't do it. 'Cause I realized my little waitress Roxanne was still inside closing up. Little Roxanne. Sweet Roxanne. Hell, Roxanne's a hot little girl. She could see what I needed and she was willing to give it to me. So—I parked my car behind the grill. We crawled in the back seat and I looked up and winked at this big black ugly moon hangin' up there laughing at me!

Master Of The Obvious

Kevin Fisher

Scene: here and now

Dramatic
Father: a man recalling the traumatic birth of his first child, 30s

Childbirth isn't always a walk in the park, as women know all too well. Here, a new father reveals his own struggle to cope with his wife's compromised labor.

FATHER: My pregnant wife calls . They have her at the hospital and they won't let her leave…For the first and only time in my life, I take a cab five blocks. They have her on a monitor that spikes when the contractions are coming so I can lean over my sweating wife and tell her "Its coming" and she can say *"I know."* Parents are about the worst people you'd ever want to meet. They all say, "well it'll change your life" and I always say "no it won't." and they say "yes it will" and I say "No it won't." until they give up and I'm left to talk to the single people. Single people *without* pets. We'd gone to Bradley. Which is Lamaze without ridiculous hyperventilating. Bradley presents a view of natural childbirth that we later realized was pure fantasy. Mothers through back massage and creative visualizations—"de sand is warm, the Caribbean water laps at your feet, you are on vacation"—are supposed to be able to give birth without any pain medication whatsoever. Dr. Bradley says that mothers who take pain killers during birth are giving their babies *cocaine.* I'd like to hear his thoughts on prostrate surgery. A friend of mine from college inherited his family farm. The one time I visited we went out looking for a lost pregnant cow. It was almost dark when I found her in a pouring cold rain. She was lying on her side, covered in mud, breathing hard, drooling white foam. The calf's head was sticking out dead. My friend went to get the vet, and told me I had to get the cow up on her feet or she'd die. So he gave me the cattle prod, and for the next hour and a half I try to coax the cow to get up with words, and eventually the electric cattle prod. The vet comes and we pull out the dead calf and ten feet of placenta. And my friend shoots the cow because she's paralyzed. But he doesn't tell me he's going to do this, he just says "stand back" and I hear this bang and I get hit with blood. This was my only *prior* birth experience. After twelve hours at the hospital, my wife's only contracted a bit, they want to put her on the "pit." The "pit" is a drip IV of a drug that accelerates contractions. For the next five hours my wife stands bent over. She doesn't talk and she looks like she's nine years old and she's experiencing over and over watching her favorite dog being hit by a car again every twenty seconds. We do not speak except when she starts to get these fierce shakes on top of the contractions, and I hear her whisper "Pet me like a cat." And climbing over the tubes and monitor and the nurses, I do. I've never seen anyone really experience pain like this. After five hours, my wife says "Give me the epidural." They tap into her spine and for the first time in hours we talk. They check her and she's over half dilated, and so they want to break her water to push things along. And they use what looks like a knitting needle, and I ask her how it feels and she says "like having someone scrape your bones with a cheese grater." We have two good hours, but the fetal heartbeat is really high. No one tells us this but we can read the monitor and its at 180 beats a minute. And the Doctor comes in to say we have to go off the pit to slow the heartbeat. And they take her off the pit, and everyone leaves. And I remember someone telling us, that you know you're in trouble if they start disappearing, because no one wants to be in the room when something goes wrong. Then the heartbeat goes to 209 a minute. A few days later after we were home, I found a metronome and I set it at 209. Its prestissimo. As fast as music will go. Right now, my wife and I look at each other and know both we can't go there. Everyone has a dead baby or a umbilical cord story they have to tell you. My response, if someone starts to tell me about some umbilical cord that acts

73

like a malevolent garden hose, I say "that's ok…we're having one of the new cordless babies." Someone tells us that more hermaphrodite babies are being born. And in the old days the doctor would flip a coin and decide the sex, but now you have to wait till they're old enough to make an informed choice. Assuming they don't want the flexibility. Until then names are a problem. My wife says she wants a C section *now*. They take her away to the O.R. I suit up in a green paper suit, but before they let me in to see my wife who's in the O.R., the nurses tell me I have to check out of our room. I throw my wife's clothes into the hallway and run to the O.R. In the operating room, I crouch next to my wife as she lies on the operating table. A curtain separates her head and where the doctor's work. And we pretend she's not being operated on, but instead she's *merely* trapped under a crane or a train or a building and we're waiting for the rescue team. After a while the doctor tells me to look and I look and a purplish head and body comes out of a hole in my wife's stomach…like a roll of cookie dough with eyes. I wait to leave until my wife is off her oxygen mask. They want me to leave earlier, but I keep coming back and they give up. Some young guy who arrives with flowers after visiting hours and wants to see one of the mothers on the floor. And they won't let him in even though he tells them he's the father. And the way he says it its like the first time he said it and its a big deal confession, and they still won't let him in and he leaves and I wonder if he's ever coming back. At three in the morning, I go by the nursery on my way home and its empty except for a mid-aged nurse holding up a loud screaming baby by one leg as she washes it and I realize that's my daughter. And I feel scared. And maybe I should go in and take her from the nurse and wash her myself, but I don't because she looks like a small animal, a small feral scary animal. Having kids was sort of a leap of faith. Parents keep saying you're going to love them because they're so helpless. Because they need you. I never got this because I don't like needy people. Somehow I didn't experience that moment I was supposed to have in the operating room—which everyone says happens—when you look into your daughter's eyes and you get it. You suddenly understand your place in the universe. I realize I'm not ready, and so I go home, and its quiet there for what I later realized was the last time, and I pour myself a stiff drink and read Dr. Spock, but unlike the other Spock this one has little to say about my place in the universe.

Molly Sweeny

Brian Friel

Scene: Ireland

Serio-comic
Frank: a man trying to help his blind wife to see the world, 40s

> *Here, Frank recalls the first time he asked Molly out on a date.*

FRANK: I spent a week in the library—the week after I first met her—one full week immersing myself in books and encyclopedias and magazines and articles—anything, everything I could find about eyes and vision and eye diseases and blindness. Fascinating. I can't tell you—fascinating. I look out of my bed-room window and at a single glance I see the front garden and the road beyond and cars and buses and the tennis courts on the far side and people playing on them and the hills beyond that. Everything—all those details and dozens more—all seen in one immediate, comprehensive perception. But Molly's world isn't perceived instantly, comprehensively. She composes a world from a sequence of impressions; one after the other, in time. For example, she knows that this is a carving knife because first she can feel the handle; then she can feel this long blade; then this sharp edge. In sequence. In time. What is this object? These are ears. This is a furry body. Those are paws. That is a long tail. Ah, a cat! In sequence. Sequentially. Right? Right. Now a personal question. You are going to ask this blind lady out for an evening. What would be the ideal entertainment for somebody like her? A meal? A concert? A walk? Maybe a swim? Billy Hughes says she's a wonderful swimmer. *(He shakes his head slowly.)* The week in the library pays off. Know the answer instantly. Dancing. Take her dancing. With her disability the perfect, the absolutely perfect relaxation. Forget about space, distance, who's close, who's far,

76

who's approaching. Forget about time. This is not a sequence of events. This is one continuous, delightful event. Nothing leads to nothing else. There is only now. There is nothing subsequent. I am your eyes, your ears, your location, your sense of space. Trust me. Dancing. Obvious. Straight into a phone-box and asked her would she come with me to the Hikers Club dance the following Saturday. It'll be small, I said; more like a party. What do you say? Silence. We'll ask Billy and Rita and we'll make it a foursome and we'll have our own table and our own fun. Not a word. Please, Molly. In my heart of hearts I really didn't think she'd say yes. For God's sake why should she? Middle-aged. No skill. No job. No prospect of a job. Two rooms above Kelly's cake shop. And not exactly Rudolf Valentino. And when she did speak, when she said very politely, "Thank you, Frank. I'd love to go," do you know what I said? "All right then." Bloody brilliant! But I vowed to myself in that phone-box, I made a vow there and then that at the dance on Saturday night I wouldn't open the big mouth— big?—enormous for Christ's sake!—I wouldn't open it once all night, all week. Talking of Valentino, in point of fact Valentino was no Adonis himself. Average height; average looks; mediocre talent. And if he hadn't died so young—in 1926—he was only thirty-one—and in those mysterious circumstances that were never fully explained—he would never have become the cult fig-ure the studios worked so hard to…Anyhow…

Naked Mole Rats
In The World Of Darkness
Michael T. Folie

Scene: the Bronx Zoo

Dramatic
Jack: a man suffering from a mid-life crisis, 40s

Here, Jack describes his unhappy state to his wife, Barbara.

JACK: Light! Barbara, I want…I need light.
    [BARBARA: Light? You want light?]
JACK: Yes.
    [BARBARA: You're leaving us for light? I've heard a lot of kooky
    reasons for divorce, Jack, but insufficient lighting…]
JACK: That's not what I…
    [BARBARA: I mean, if more light is all you want we can stop at
    Sears on the way home. You want light, they got light.]
JACK: Not that kind of light! Real light. Sunlight. My life used to
be filled with light, Babs. I could see. See where I was going.
Now. I leave the house, it's dark. I come home. It's dark. I spend
my days in a neon-lit black box on a grid. Neon isn't light. Neon
sucks light out of you. My whole life is nothing but rooting
around in the dark, grubbing for a living with other creatures as
blind and useless as myself. *(Pause.)* I was going to make people
see! Don't you remember? That's what I set out to do. I was
going to take the world around me—the visible world; the *invis-
ible*—and make people see it. Really see it! And what do I do? I'm
in advertising, Babs. Product packaging. My job is to fool people.
To make them see what's not there. To blind them to what is
there. I take all of the talent I was born with, I take all of the techniques I learned in school, techniques…techniques developed by
Turner, by Carravagio, by Monet; men who were gods! Men who
dedicated their lives bringing the light of God down to earth and

putting it on canvas; and I use all of that to sell soap! *(Pause.)* Don't you see? I have become everything I ever hated about this world. *(Pause.)* I'm no good to you this way, Barbara. I'm no damn good. To you. To my children. I'm a failure. Worse than a failure. I am a totally corrupt person. And I have to leave. *(Pause.)* Good bye. *(Pause. He doesn't move.)*

Old Wicked Songs

Jon Marans

Scene: Vienna, 1986

Dramatic
Stephan Hoffman: an American music student, 25

> *The former child prodigy has traveled to Vienna to study piano. Before he may study with Professor Schiller, however, he must first study singing with the eccentric professor Mashkan. Stephan, who is Jewish, assumes that Mashkan is an anti-Semite based upon the old man's caustic commentary. Here, Stephan angrily tells Mashkan of his weekend visit to Dachau just prior to discovering the telltale tattoo on the professor's arm.*

STEPHEN: *(Serious again.)* Two weeks ago, I took the train to Munich. The next morning I took another train from Munich to Dachau—

[MASHKAN: I do not want—]

STEPHEN: —I arrived at the station fairly early, assuming the ride would take a while. It took twenty minutes. Isn't that interesting? Only twenty minutes from the heart of Munich to Dachau.

[MASHKAN: I think *I'll* have some coffee.]

STEPHEN: At first, I thought I was on the wrong train. So I turned to an older woman sitting next to me and asked her in German if this was the way to Dachau.

[MASHKAN: Actually, if you'd like some coffee—]

STEPHEN: And she said to me "I knew nothing that went on there!" From the train, I took a short bus ride to the camp. On the bus, a young woman in front of me turned around and said "What are you doing here?!" I told her, "I'm here to see Dachau." She asked 'why?' and I said *(Stammering.)* "because it's important for people to see this place." And she said, "but why do *you* want to see it?!" And I said "because I'm Jewish." And then she said, *(Very casually.)* "well why didn't you say so in the first place?" Then she told me to move over—and sat next to me. Her name was Sarah. She grew up in Israel. Her grandparents had been in Dachau. They didn't want her to see it. Together, she and I did. It's funny. I was prepared for the *"Arbeit Macht Frei"* sign, the barbed wire fences, the guard posts. I wasn't prepared for how beautifully Dachau had been fixed up. No, covered over. Most of the buildings—gone. Those that were left—white-washed. The grass—so green. A stream near the side of the camp had a quaint little bridge. If I hadn't known better, I'd never suspect these few acres of land had been crowded with thousand of emaciated, tortured bodies. There was a small museum which told "the story"—mostly through pictures. And under each picture, a description. The only problem—the descriptions were in German—*no* translations. So most people there couldn't read it since German was not the predominant language among visitors. For those of us who could read the captions, they supplied only the barest of facts. As I walked through, I was silent. Stunned. Feeling—numb from the experience. Not Sarah. She was enraged. I could see her whole body tightening up as we walked from room to room in the museum. Finally, we passed a guard and she started yelling at him, saying he was burying the truth!...And the whole time he just stood there expressionless—silent. After that, we saw the crematorium. Sarah cried. I couldn't. I was too angry. And confused. Before leaving, we saw the Israeli Memorial. It's a stone tower. You look into it by going down a ramp and peering through a gate. Inside, it's almost completely dark except for a small beam of light that shines down from the top...a single beam of light surrounded by darkness. You can't go inside the memorial. The gate's locked. On the way out of the camp, we picked up a brochure—*this* one in English—telling us to "please stroll through the lovely *town* of Dachau after leaving." We didn't. For some reason, the Bavarian charm was lost on us. That evening, we spent a quiet dinner together. At the end of the main course, Sarah asked if I would spend the

81

night with her. Back at her hotel room we made love. *(Surprised, embarrassed.)* It was hot. Really hot. For hours and hours into the night. And then again the next morning. And I kept thinking, "why is this so special? Because she's Jewish? Or because of what happened at Dachau? Or is she just great in bed? Or am I suddenly better in bed? And then it hit me— *(Not pleased.)* You were right. That combination of sadness and joy. With one emotion heightened, so is the other. The next afternoon, she caught her train to Prague. And these last two weeks, I've wandered through Vienna, "the city of dreams." And every time I turned and saw a beautiful bridge or a quaint babbling brook, I broke into a sweat. And every time I got off the U-bahn and heard that recorded message 'End of the line, everybody off,' I felt sick to my stomach. And thought of a man I had respected. Once. *(He starts gathering up his music.)*

An Ordinary Woman Under Stress

Sandra Marie Vago

Scene: a bar in Chicago

Dramatic
Jake: a bar owner, 57

> *Here, Jake tells the story of his brief and unhappy marriage to a stranger.*

JAKE: I had…or should I say, my wife of eight months had a lovely little girl during our short lived marriage.

[SARAH: It's none of my business.]

JAKE: Please, allow me to bore you for just a moment. *(He gets himself a beer.)* That's the reason she married me. We'd had a…tryst? Is that the right word? Maybe not. A tryst refers to a meeting between two lovers and lovers we were not! I guess it was more of a sexual consolation…yes, that would better describe it, and I was the consolation prize. Not exactly like winning the lottery, getting me. *(He laughs and stops a moment.)* You see, her lover, my best friend, Jack, he was killed…Vietnam… one month before he was due to be discharged.

[SARAH: I'm sorry…]

JAKE: She was in pain. For that matter, I was in pain. Add to that the fact that I had always been a wee bit in love with her myself and it was the first time she'd ever really needed *me.* We got together and…unfortunately, she got pregnant. *(He stops and takes a drink.)* We were married almost on the exact day her wedding to Jack was scheduled to take place. Big mistake!

[SARAH: Listen…I…uh, I shouldn't…]

JAKE: No, please, I'd like you to know. I don't even know why, I've never told anyone…I just wanna tell you, now. *(Beat.)* Six months after the wedding, Jackie was born, Myra packed their bags one day and went back to her parents.

[SARAH: She just took the baby and left?]

(He stops and picks up the mask.)

JAKE: I'm making her sound cold, my young bride. Nothing could be further from the truth. She was warm, beautiful and vulnerable. And she was very much in love, but not with me. It wasn't her fault...it wasn't even mine. If anything was to blame it was the war and simple human frailty. We all make mistakes. I'm just sorry that ours had to affect our child...Myra let me visit and my daughter and I became friends. I still see her when I can. *(He finishes his beer.)* No, she was not cold, my young bride, just very, very sad.

Painting X's On The Moon

Richard Vetere

Scene: Queens

Dramatic
Lou Barbota: handsome Queens gangster; intelligent and dangerous, 30s

> *Lou is being sent to prison for fifteen years. Knowing that he won't survive without his wife, Diane, he summons artist Nick Dante to one of his illegal garbage dumps and demands that Nick paint a portrait of Diane.*

LOU: I coped a plea. With my record, they could have put me away for a very long time. But instead, I keep the place running, I bring in more dumpers and I look at fifteen. For ratting-out my partners I cut ten years off my sentence. Since they weren't connected guys, the boys upstairs gave me the okay.

[NICK DANTE: What do you want from me?]

LOU: Diane, you know, she goes out there to her paradise and pretends that I am just a part of her past. Everything is fine for awhile until one night she wakes up in a sweat. She looks around at her fake palms trees and her actor's headshot and she realizes that she will disappear. That town doesn't give a shit about her. She will be replaced next week because out there they have no memory. So, she gets on a plane and gets back here where she knows Lou can take her in his arms. Lou makes her pain go away. Do you know why? Because I see through her make up. *I see her,* pal. I can stay up all night and live with no sleep, just like her. When she burns down the night, I'm right there with her. And when it gets too dark for her, it's me, Lou, who curses everything she's afraid of.

[NICK DANTE: *(Bewildered.)* Why are you telling me this? Why are you telling me this *now?*]

LOU: Because the day after tomorrow they are locking me up for a long time.

[NICK DANTE: I thought you had—sophisticated ways of making money. But I never expected this...So, you made millions...]

LOU: And not just from here. I got another dump up near Albany. And another in Rhode Island. I got partners on those, too. At one of my dumps they build a mall. Problem is the gas fumes from the waste put half the neighborhood in the hospital. *(Pause.)* Right now you are thinking, what kind of monster is this character, right?

[NICK DANTE: Something like that.]

LOU: Sure, think that self righteous crap if it makes you feel better. You can do that, too, because you're down here, pal, you're one of the nobody's. But once you raise your head up and try to make the world work for you, you find out they got all kinds of rules. And who are they? They are those who got. And they got *big*. I'm nobody compared to them. And they run everything. And the thing they fear most is anybody getting up there where they are—black or white. So, they give you things to keep you quiet. They sedate your appetite. "Here, you can run some gambling joints, you can own a crack house, you can push a couple of hookers." But the minute you show any real brains, any real ambition, they go after you with everything they got! The FBI, CIA, everything. They make the laws for themselves. They put amendments to the constitution! They have the power. *(A beat.)* They start wars and burn innocent people and then they turn around to guys like me and say, "Hey, you are getting our kids high on drugs!" They take what they want anywhere in the world, but when I want to run a little dump site they come around and start taking pictures. Did you see Reagan go to jail for dealing arms to the Iranians? Did Bush, no? They killed Kennedy and whoever got their names? They are the big fish and they don't fry in anybody's pan. All they talk about is building new prisons to put the little fish in. Well, Nick, this is all they let me have and I took it! I'm the barbarian at their gate. *(Pause.)* I hate

86

this place. But I come here every night and I watch it. I share it with the rats and I hate it. But I endure it because I stand here and I think of Diane. I think of how pretty she is and how people fantasize about her and then I say, "She's yours, Lou." And then this place don't seem so ugly anymore. *(Pause.)* I don't care how much art I own—those wealthy louses in their highrisers across the river see me as subhuman. I know that. They call me names, and then they get the government to do their dirty work.

    [NICK DANTE: Why am I out here?]

LOU: Because I'm not going to make it through the fifteen, Nick. Without her near me, I'll never make it inside.

    [NICK DANTE: Then there's nothing you can do...]

LOU: You can help me. You're the only one. Whatever you want from me, whatever you need—it's yours.

    [NICK DANTE: What do you want me to do?]

LOU: Capture on your canvas, for all time, my love for my wife.

Painting X's On The Moon

Richard Vetere

Scene: Queens

Dramatic
Charlie: a gangster's bodyguard; an abuser of women, 30s

When young Stephanie makes herself a gangster's whore by throwing herself at Charlie, he responds with acid misogynistic insight.

CHARLIE: Hey, look, talk about something else, okay? I mean, you talk like a kid. You stop being a kid and maybe you'll find a guy who will be nice to you and won't lie or cheat or curse. But you know something? There ain't any guys like that. Not any guy with looks, brains, or money. The only kind of guys who are like the type you are talking about, are guys who are eighty with one foot in the grave. Maybe! Maybe you will find the guy on a respirator.

[STEPHANIE: You are sadistic.]

CHARLIE: Young girls. They want perfection. All they want is what they think they deserve. Where do you get these ideas about men? In books? The movies? Come on, maybe some guy out there is loyal and true blue and dead below the belly button, but let me tell you this—a young girl like you would kill him in a week. You would devastate him. You would have him on his knees! Women think they bring compassion to the world. What bullshit! What nonsense!

Portrait Of The Virgin Mary Feeding The Dinosaurs

Jeff Goode

Scene: a wilderness

Serio-comic
Mephistopheles: a devilish guy

Here, a waggish Mephistopheles mocks the Ten Commandments.

MEPHISTOPHELES: How would you like a moral dilemma? *(Moses Impression. Commanding voice.) Thou shalt not kill.* That's right, *I* don't want you to kill. I am asking you, pleading with you not to kill. It accomplishes so little. He or she is dead, and you probably go to jail for the rest of your life, and who does that leave to play with me? No, no, absolutely no killing. If it's not all-out genocide I don't wanna hear about it. And I am absolutely against abortion. What good does that do? *(Sharing a delicious, malicious secret.)* Far better to let it live, grow up, have a miserable childhood, "Where's your father?" "I don't have a father." "Hahahahaha," hopefully it lives in poverty, so it turns to the streets, to a life of crime, so it develops a healthy lack of respect for other people's earthly possessions. Yes. Steals a car. Assault, maybe. Sells drugs to confused children from *good* families. Then, after eighteen to twenty years of mayhem, *then* let it commit some horrible atrocity which demands the death penalty. Oh, I'm very much in favor of capital punishment. Exodus 7:18 "An eye for an eye." The more eyes, the better! Hell, anytime I can *pull someone's eyeball out of its socket in the name of God...*I'm in Heaven...so to speak. That's why I like 'feel good' movies. *Do not steal! (Looking for it on his tablet.)* "Thou shalt not steal," it says that here somewhere. And I support that one hundred percent. Don't steal. It's tacky. Better to trick them into *giving* you their money. Better to *borrow* from them and never give it back.

89

Better to break the things they have and let them keep them. I'd rather have an inside trader than a carjacker. I'd rather have a computer pirate than a purse-snatcher. I'd rather have one white collar criminal working for me than *ten* thugs, robbers and thieves. Wouldn't you? *(Getting fired up.)* I mean, come on, people, we gotta think in terms of job efficiency, here. I don't have time to quibble about— *(Picks a sin from his tablet at random.)* —coveting your neighbor's wife. Fine, don't do it. Just *tell* everybody you fucked her and I'm happy. It causes the same amount of interpersonal anguish *more* really, and it takes less time, less effort. Efficiency. Okay, end of sermon. You wanna see my Moses impression?

Sad Laughter

Charles Deemer

Scene: here and now

Serio-comic
The Ghost of Moliere

> *Here, the timeless playwright addresses his future audiences.*

MOLIERE: Shed no tears! You rot in one grave as another;
If you don't believe that, don't ever have a mother.
The luck that gets us all got me—
Though I'm better off than most, you must agree.
Consider this: though I am dust, you're glad to pay
Right through the nose to see my plays!
Without me, Montfleury's just a name;
Because of me, he has a kind of fame.
The Archibishop of Paris is no concern of yours
Except for me—I give him the notoriety he deserves.
In other words, why shed a tear for me?
My plays live on until eternity!
Oh, I know—in your age the time is getting short,
Everywhere there's war, famine, a great environmental wart.
Yet you insist your own age is unique:
"Never has civilization reached such a peak!"
But I question this wisdom found on TV and in "Forbes,"
Though maybe that's presumptuous, coming from a corpse.
Still, I don't see our times as different, I confess,
Since in your age, as in mine, it's all a mess.
Though you've reached the moon, discovered strange galactic
    gasses,
Three hundred years later, the world's still full of asses!
    (La Grange enters.)

[LA GRANGE: So we hope we've moved you and given you a little fun; In truth...]

MOLIERE AND LA GRANGE: there's not a damn thing new beneath the sun.

(Music fanfare and curtain call: the play is over.)

Shylock

Mark Leiren-Young

Scene: a stage

Serio-comic

Jon Davies: an actor concerned with the preservation of all of Shakespeare's works, whether politically correct or not, 40s

> *When his performance as Shylock meets with pubic outrage, Jon (who is Jewish) examines the character both within and without its historical and cultural context. Here, Jon recalls his first encounter with the Bard of Avon.*

JON DAVIES: I fell in love with Shakespeare for the stories. Not the words. When I visited my grandmother at the home, when I was a kid, I always used to stare at her bookshelf, which was mostly cluttered up with pictures of family, photo albums, and three books: the Torah, that's the old testament—a prayer book and Shakespeare. It had well-worn red leather bindings and the spine had an etching of a man's face, Shakespeare's face, although I didn't know that at the time. I thought it was a picture of a sorcerer, perhaps even Merlin. And I thought the book was a collection of magic spells. My grandmother was so old that for all I knew she used to be friends with Merlin. So on my thirteenth birthday my Grandmother gave me her copy of *The Collected Works* and I was delighted. Until I went into my bedroom with my new treasure, opened it up and discovered it was just a bunch of stupid, boring plays written in very strange English. There weren't even any pictures. I was heartbroken. The closest I got to "literature" was Batman. So I put the book on my shelf and I probably would have forgotten all about it if not for a severe case of the measles about a year later. It took me two days to reread all my comic books. On day three I started *King Lear.* I didn't understand all the words, I didn't understand most of the words, but somehow I managed to understand the story because at about midnight on day four—as Lear cradled his poor, lifeless Cordelia in his arms—I began to cry. And it was the first time a story in a book ever made me cry. There were no spells—unless you count the incantations from the Scottish play—but it was magic all the same. Unlike Loffleur, I fell in love with Shakespeare for the stories. But the words came a close second. They may not taste like champagne or chocolate—not to me anyway—but there's something very...fulfilling...about speaking them. They make me feel like the dream-speaker of the tribe, like I'm seeing something that may be or ought to be or simply was and shouldn't be forgotten. Fulfilling. More fulfilling than that allergy commercial I did a few months ago. You know the one. Except the allergy commercial paid more than a full season at the festival. So when the Festival approached me about playing Shylock, Tony and I talked about the play and agreed—this would be an attempt to do Shylock the way he was written. So instead of starting with Jew—I started with villain. Instead of starting with outcast, I started with greed. And vengeance. And the type of villain Shakespeare's audience would have hated and booed and hissed. Much the same way some people in the audience for this show have hated and booed and hissed. The type of villain Shakespeare actually wrote. Yes, a negative character. So I started my research. I looked at the great Shylocks in history. At Macklin and Kean and the others who had played him through the ages. And all the greats had started with the same impulse—either a clown, who the world would laugh at, or a tragic and sympathetic old man. A man worn down by the wrongs of society. A man the audience could pity and perhaps even love because, Christmas pantomimes aside, all actors want to be loved. But almost all these men ultimately changed their approach. The longer they played the role the more apparent it became that Shylock isn't a wronged hero or a pathetic old man—he's supposed to be the villain. And maybe there are moments the audience is supposed to feel for him, but no more than they're supposed to briefly feel for Richard the Third. If Shakespeare truly meant to create a story about a sympathetic Jew, if he truly wanted to create a plea for tolerance, surely he wouldn't have told the story of a cruel Jewish moneylender who lives for vengeance. Moneylender—a profession lower on the social ladder in his day than prostitute. Or actor. Any man who could create moments of sympathy for Richard the Third could surely have come up with a more appealing and honourable Jew than Shylock the moneylender, Shylock the fiend. If he wanted us to accept the Jew as human, why praise Jessica for her "Christian temperament." Why abuse and humiliate Shylock and demand that he convert?

Six At Twenty Six

Seth Kramer

Scene: here and now

Dramatic

Abe: a man suffering from Alzheimer's Disease, 70.

> *Abe is in the beginning stages of Alzheimer's. Here, he muses about a photograph he keeps in his wallet.*

> *(Abe sits alone in a spot.)*

ABE: I have this picture. I know it's mine because I keep it in my wallet. It's an old black and white of me holding a fish. The fish is a pike that runs the length of my entire arm—beautiful and sleek and long. In the picture I'm a lot younger, a chubby face that is beaming from ear to ear. The lake in the background is good old lake Oka-Bodgi. Next to me stands a man in knee high boots wearing a pair of old fashioned suspender pants. He has a hat tipped back on his head, his hand resting on my shoulder and his face is split by this crooked grin of pride. I've looked and looked and looked… *(Reaching inside.)* Studied every inch of that picture, I keep expecting to see something in those black and white eyes—something I'll know. The way his hand felt, the slant of his smile…but nothing ever comes. *(Pause.)* I keep a black and white stranger with me at all times in my wallet. I don't think I'll ever never know his name again.

> *(Blackout.)*

Six At Twenty Six

Seth Kramer

Scene: here and now

Dramatic
Abe: a man suffering from Alzheimer's Disease, 70.

Here, Abe seems to have found an odd and unsettling peace with his infirmity.

(Abe sits alone in a spot. He is perfectly lucid and peaceful.)
ABE: A world without memory is a world of the present. The past exists only in books, in documents. In order to know himself, each person carries his own Book of Life, which is filled with the history of his life. With time, each person's Book of Life thickens until it can not be read in one sitting. And then comes a choice—accept the burden of time or abandon the past. Without his Book of Life, a person is a snapshot, a two dimensional image, a ghost. It matters not if yesterday they were rich or poor, educated or ignorant, proud or humble, in love or empty-hearted—no more than it matters how a soft wind gets into their hair. Such people look you directly in the eye and grip your hand firmly. Such people walk with the limber strides of their youth. For it is only habit and memory that dulls our passions. Without memory each night is the first night. Each morning, the first morning, and each kiss stolen for the first time. In a world without memory.
(Blackout.)

Slaughter City

Naomi Wallace

Scene: Slaughter City, USA

Dramatic
Brandon: a young worker in a slaughterhouse, 20s

> *As he shows a new worker how to pull loins, Brandon details his history at the slaughterhouse*

BRANDON: When I started working here, I vomited every Monday morning. They dropped me down on the kill floor pulling black guts and cleaning chitterlings. Hog shit in my nose, in my mouth, all day long. Then I was trimming jaw bones. Lost a thumb, see? Moving up. Moving up in the pay bracket. Ten cents more. Fifteen cents more. All the time waiting to get to the knives. Then I was head boner. Slipped a disk twice. Twenty-five cents more. Then moving up again to a scalder. Forty cents. Then forty-five. Hot. That was too damn hot. Then I was bung dropper. Too fucking intimate, cutting the assholes out of hogs. One guy slipped his bung and cut my left thigh to the bone. Then I was splitter. Top rate bracket. Bingo. New used car. Two-bedroom apartment, one for me, one for my television. I like it. I like the money.

Slaughter City

Naomi Wallace

Scene: Slaughter City, USA

Dramatic
Tuck: a supervisor in the slaughterhouse, 40s

> *Tuck, who is black, here derides Cod, a new employee in the slaughterhouse, for being Irish.*

TUCK: In Latin your name is Gadus *morrhua*. Don't you think Gadus has just a bit more status to it? And status—might be what a guy like you needs, Gadus. Gadus?

[COD: Yeah.]

TUCK: You missed a bit. To your left. *(Beat.)* Did you know you were once thought of as a nigger, Gadus? Now don't take offense. I know white folks don't like being called nigger. It gets them confused. *(Beat.)* Why are you making those puny strokes. Watch me. *(Tuck takes the broom and makes some masterful and fancy sweeps with it.)* History, Gadus. You ever read? That's where you'll find the key. *(Tuck gives Cod back the broom.)* When you Irishmen carne over here in the 1800s, after that British potato problem, you were called a dark race, low browed and savage. Oh yeah. You were more feared than us blacks. You were the Celtic Beast and you chased the women and raped the chickens. That's a fact. You lived side by side with us in the slums. Chums we were, you and me. Chummed up and slumming it together. Then you were given a raise. That raise was the right to call us nigger and the right not to be called a nigger yourself. So you see, whiteness don't have to be a colour, Gadus. It can be a wage. *(Watching him sweep.)* That's it. Use your shoulders. Pull and push. Pull and push.

Smoke & Mirrors

Eric C. Peterson

Scene: here and now

Dramatic
Tom: a man who uses women, 30s

> *Apparently, there aren't enough women in town to satisfy Tom's needs. Here, he describes what is, unfortunately, a typical night in his life.*

> *(Tom stands alone in the spotlight and addresses the audience.)*

TOM: Real late last night…I went over to see Simone. We had a fight…pretty bad. And of course *I'm* always the one who has to apologize, so…what the hell, right? I was also feeling a little horny, and an apology is usually a good way to get laid, so…I go over there, and I'm in the hallway, and I can hear her three doors down just throwing shit all over the place. She's screaming and glass is breaking, and this old lady that lives next door has got her door open and is about to call the police, but I stop her. I tell her I'll take care of it. That old lady loves me, man…So, anyway, I knock on her door…She doesn't hear me. So I start pounding. Eventually, she comes to the door, cracks it open. I couldn't see much, but holy Christ…her place was completely trashed, and she had blood all over her hands. She looked up at me, and smiled. Well, it wasn't really a smile, it was more of a…grimace…or something. I looked down at her, and said, "I'm sorry." She said, "Yeah, okay," and then she shut the door in my face. I waited a while, and listened. Couldn't hear a damn thing, so I knocked on the door again. She opened it up again, all angry and shit, and says, "What do you want now?!" I told her I'd help her clean up, and she smiled again, and said…"I wish you could."

Then she shut the door again. I could hear her crying. I didn't want to be an asshole and just leave, but…there's just no dealing with Simone when she's in one of those moods. So I went down to a pay phone and called Elizabeth. I told her to meet me at my place. When I got home, she was there waiting for me. She lives all the way across town, and dammit if she didn't beat me home. She wanted it bad…After it was over, I got up…rolled over. She propped herself up on her elbow, and looked down at me. She said, "I love you." I usually hate it when she says that, but…right about that time, it was…nice to hear.

(Lights fade.)

The Souvenir Of Pompeii

Sari Bodi

Scene: here and now

Dramatic
Sam: a man whose wife has just kidnapped a baby from the hospital, 30–40

> *When Helen disappears with another woman's child, Sam must do his best to answer questions about her motives and possible whereabouts.*

SAM: I don't know where Helen is. I'm not hiding her. I wouldn't keep a baby that wasn't mine. I'm too honest. I was brought up to believe that if I worked hard, was nice to my neighbors, and gave money to charity, my life would run smoothly. Just this morning when I was at the supermarket, a woman asked me to feed the homeless. Which I did, literally. You actually slip your money into the mouth of a plastic homeless person. It was a bit off-putting at first, but actually quite satisfying. And I thought that that act would put me in good stead with the Fates. But it didn't. Because when I got back from the supermarket, Helen is sitting in the kitchen trying to feed milk to a baby. "This is Pericles," she says. "The child we created last night." And she is so convinced, that for a split second I wonder if I remembered to buy baby food. "Helen, this is not our baby," I say. The baby starts to scream. "We need to find its mother, Helen. Where did you get her? Do I have to call the police?" "You want to give your child to the police?" she says. "How silly, Sam. After all the time we've spent trying to create her." I do want a child. When we were first married, Helen and I would imagine ourselves as a mother hen and a rooster with a brood of chicks following us wherever we went. But now when I see the children on the block running after the ice cream truck, I imagine that the Good Humor man is the

Pied Piper who will pack them all up in the truck, and unfreeze them only after I am dead. Helen thinks her fertility problem stems from a prehistoric biological problem. That a woman in the cave days who had her high level of anxiety would have been prevented from releasing eggs because it meant that wild animals were nearby which might devour the newborn. But she has a new historical theory every month. And none of them work. And do you know why? Because Helen and I have bad luck. That's all it is. Bad luck. And there is nothing you can do about that. Not even steal a baby. Which is probably the worst crime anyone could commit. And I tell Helen this while the baby is screaming. Which probably wasn't the right thing to do because Helen grabbed the baby and ran. I was left holding the milk carton. I had to call the police. And well, here you are. You probably have children of your own, don't you? You'll leave here, and go home to a house full of screaming kids. Wonderfully screaming kids. And we'll be left here—with the quiet.

Tell Me What You Want

Robert Coles

Scene: here and now

Dramatic
Landon: a poet, 20s–30s

Here, Landon reveals his sense of alienation as he describes his disassociative feelings about sex.

LANDON: I walk the cold indifferent blocks of the city's night. Gritty sidewalks, their surfaces oozing carelessness, disinterest and accident. Papers dropped, then smeared with oil, excrement, blood. Gray to purple to black to gray to purple to black. All the colors of our bodies and our lives mix together on these streets to produce only three shades. Gray to purple to black to gray to purple to black. I count the colors as I walk. Looking down. Only down. The pavement is my vista. A landscape of our existence upon the concrete. Things cast off from our flesh and our consumption. This is the meat market—At morning the carcasses hang, and by night the bodies thrash together. I walk these blocks, on a certain night at a certain time. I walk. I speed. I have a destination. A purpose. I go to the place where the bodies thrash. Thrash. Grab. Pound. Throb. Pretend. Finish. I go there. I thrash. I pretend. I finish. I leave. Mission accomplished. Nothing to be ashamed of, nothing to be proud of. I am indifferent to it. As the city's night is indifferent to me. I walk back, through those coarse streets, and as I go I count the colors on the sidewalks. Only three. Papers dropped, wrappers flung away. The torn coatings of our momentary absorption. We finished them and tossed aside the waste. Finished. Wasted. Mashed together with all our other excrement. So many colors turned to three. Gray to purple to black. The pavement of the meat market is my landscape, and I am as indifferent to it as it is to me.

Tuesday

Paul Mullin

Scene: a psychiatric hospital

Dramatic
Audie: a man suffering from a memory disorder, 40s

Brought on by chronic alcohol abuse and exacerbated by head trauma, Audie's Korsakoff's Syndrome manifests itself in the patient as the inability to remember anything that happened the day before. Part of Audie's therapy has been to read from prepared scripts which retell certain events in his life. Here, he forces himself to read a script in which he visits his dying father in the hospital.

(Lights up on Audie talking to Cronie in the bed again.)
AUDIE: How 'bout that, Cronie? If you took every McCall in the phone book in every city in America and you added up their total net worth, I'd still be richer than all of 'em put together. Ain't that a bitch? Audie, I don't want—"Audie"?…Listen to me. I called you Audie. That's funny, huh? Cronie, I don't want you to die, but what can I do?…You die, you take with you the moment I was conceived, or Cathy, or Kenny—all of us. Not that you probably remember—not that you probably remember much of your life… Do you remember, Cronie? The night you squirted me up inside Mom? I remember the night me and Elizabeth made Charlie. I'm not sure about Emily, but Charlie I remember. Yeah, yeah—accident: absolutely, but whatever: it was glorious. Wow! No wonder, right? No wonder there's so many of us. *(Pause.)* Dumb shit micks… Why did you do it, Audie—Cronie? Why did you bother? Why stay here nearly eighty fucking years only to die all shrunken up and dumb in some hospital bed? And don't give me that "it was a good ride, bullshit, 'cause we both know better. And so what if it was? So what if it was, huh? Do me a favor

105

when you see the old bearded bastard up there, you ask him for me—you ask him why. Why should we be grateful for all the wonderful times we have if we can't have 'em anymore? Shit, listen to me. Cursing the Lord. What would Mom say, hunh? Hell, he's probably a dumb shit mick, too. Just look around: you can tell he's a drunk. Dumb shit dumb shit dumb shit micks.
(The lights fade out.)

Twinges From The Fringe

Bob Jude Ferrante

Scene: here and now

Serio-comic
Desmond: a man with a questing mind, 20–40

> *Here, the ever-inquisitive Desmond speculates about the reality of what it must be like when an entire continent disappears.*

DESMOND: NY public library, man. NY public library. Fuckin' temple to Western culture. Stone lions, guarding undiscovered continents of knowledge and lore. Books about the *Mysteries Of The Ages.* Things that have puzzled, bewildered, confounded, confused, perplexed and posed man since the dawn of motherfucking time. Is there life after death? What is the path of righteousness? Why does the fucking clerk always put the change *on top* of the fucking bills so it slips off onto the fucking counter? I found this book: *Atlantis, The Lost Continent.* Blew my mind— *Atlantis, The Lost Continent.* But directly, directly some questions arise. OK, there was this continent called Atlantis, off the Jersey shore. Geography majors, this is how Atlantic City got its name, right? The people from Atlantis—as they are known to some, the 'Atlantis-people'—worshipped the sun. Again, just like the Jersey shore. Then it was *gone.* Now, where did it go? Guy who wrote the book asked around. Nobody knew. What about the people who invested in condos and shit? I'm talking they looked everywhere, and *nothing.* What was the explanation? "Oh, man, it's a *Mystery Of The Ages*"—which is like, complete bullshit. Imagine you go home and your apartment is gone. You ask your landlord, "where the hell is my apartment?" He says, "Hey, man, calm down, what's the matter with you, it's a *Mystery of The Ages.*" You'd have his fucking pancreas for an *hors d'oeuvre.* And the

107

pyramids. Who built these fuckers? Where are the windows? Hundreds of corner offices with no fucking windows. Give me a window, you cheap son of a bitch! Another *Mystery Of The Ages.* What is Spam made of? Luncheon meat. Like how that rolls off the tongue? Luuuncheon meeeat. Great Spam ad. "The fuck is Spam made of? A *Mystery Of The Ages.*" I don't *know* what it's made of. But I eat it. I can't help it. At the bodega, two, three in the morning. Can of Spam. One of them little one dollar and fifty cent pieces of fudge. Some pork rinds. I never eat the pork rinds. I'm saving them for Halloween. I take the pork rinds and a bottle of Elmer's glue. Two hours later I look like Job. Ring, "Trick or Treat! Gimme candy man. Glucose. Or the arms drop right off, right here on your porch." You'd be surprised how many people oblige. They cough that candy right up man. Even in August.

Visiting Mr. Green

Jeff Baron

Scene: the upper west side of Manhattan

Serio-comic
Mr. Green: a retired dry cleaner; a man hiding from life, 86

> *When Mr. Green is nearly run over by Ross, an executive with American Express, the judge sentences Ross to helping Mr. Green one day a week. After many uneasy weeks, the cantankerous Mr. Green here tells Ross the tale of how he met his beloved wife, Yetta.*

MR. GREEN: My family shared a toilet with the Garelicks, who lived next

[ROSS: This was here in New York?]

MR. GREEN: Of course New York. On Ludlow Street. *(Off Ross's blank look.)* The Lower East Side. You're supposed to be Jewish, right? So there was a toilet out in the hall, and the Garelicks— there were six of them and one boarder, and the Greens—there were six of us and no boarder—my father wouldn't have it—all thirteen people shared this one toilet. I'm twenty-five years old, I'm just getting home from work. I run up the steps cause I gotta go. I get to the toilet, and wouldn't you know it—someone's in there and someone else is waiting. The someone else who's waiting, I've never seen her before. She's the cousin of the Garelicks, seventeen years old, just arrived from Russia. She tells me this in Yiddish, by the way, because she doesn't know from English. The only thing on my mind is I gotta go, I gotta go, and wait a minute—Now *fourteen* people are gonna share this toilet? So we're waiting, we're waiting, I'm dancing, we're waiting. We keep talking, and now I'm starting to think, "This is a very nice girl." Then my brother Marvin finally comes out of the toilet. My brother Marvin, you should understand, probably didn't even have to *go*. He just liked to be alone, and in those days, the only place to be alone was the toilet. So Yetta says, in Yiddish this was, "You go ahead." And I say, "No. You were here first." And she says, "You're dancing faster. You go first." And that was it.

[ROSS: You fell in love.]

MR. GREEN: We got married six months later. Fifty-nine years we never had an argument. *(A beat.)* So...you're married?

White Men

Michael P. Scasserra

Scene: here and now

Serio-comic
The Broker: a man with a sardonic, yet practical view of life, 20–30

> *Here a young stockbroker reveals an incident from his past that changed his life.*

THE BROKER: I'll tell you what it comes down to.
Bottom line.
You want respect,
get the money.
You want people to listen to you,
to take you seriously
to whatever
da
da
da
da
da.
Get the money.
And I don't buy any bullshit about greed.
Hey
I'm self-sufficient
I don't take from you
I like to be called "sir"
and I fucking love my car phone
and I got here with nobody's help
thank you very much.
See, years ago
I didn't know what I know now.

Years ago I was stupid enough to have applied to Wharton,
right?
Best business school in the country, right?
I had the grades
I had the drive
I had the balls.
I didn't get in.
'Course when I went to my interview at Wharton
I had on the blazer
the silk tie
the button-down collar
the khakis with the cuffs
the loafers
the whole ten yards.
And I sit down in the interviewer's office
this asshole
one of these blonde
crew-cutted
you know
clean cut
chiseled features.
that Nordic woodsman by way of Yale bullshit.
Now if I had been blonde
crew-cutted
chiseled
clean-cut
da
da
da
da
da
I would've gotten in.
Irregardless
I left the asshole's office
knowing there's no way in hell he's ever gonna let me into
Wharton

112

and I'm driving home
in my Honda
I drive a BMW now
thank you very much
blue
brand new.
Irregardless
I'm driving back to New York
and some jerk-off in a Volvo
is driving the speed limit on the Garden State Parkway
like who the fuck actually drives the limit on the Parkway
so I pass him
and this piece of garbage thinks I cut him off I guess, right?
So he catches up with me
rolls down his window
looks right at me and calls me a spic.
(Pause.)
I'm Jewish.
Spic.
Can you believe that shit?
I drove up the guy's ass all the way until he exited
scared the shit out of the cock-sucker!
And that is the day I decided...
fuck Wharton.

Whiteout

Jocelyn Beard

Scene: a white supremacist compound, Idaho

Dramatic
John Creek: charismatic and dangerous leader of the Brethren, a
white supremacist militia, 50–60

> *When a plane belonging to a popular Democratic senator—
> who happens to be black—crashes on his mountain in a bliz-
> zard, Creek is astonished when the senator makes an appear-
> ance at his home to beg for help in searching for survivors
> before the FAA and authorities arrive. Creek wisely concludes
> that the small plane was carrying a passenger whose identi-
> ty could ruin the senator's career, and here takes the upper
> hand in this most volatile situation.*

CREEK: Well, isn't this a nasty little pickle that you've gotten your-
self into? You, the golden…or should I say ebony boy of the
Democratic party; not too liberal, not too conservative.
Everybody's pal on the Hill. Gonna be president someday, right
Danny Boy? Squeaky clean kid like yourself? Mr. Eagle Scout? Mr.
West Point? Sure, you smoked a little dope in college when the
rest of us were holding onto our balls in the jungle, but you sure
as hell don't smoke it now, do you, Danny Boy? No sir, not Mr.
Family Values. You leave Rebecca and kids back home in New
York? Sure you did. They just would have been in the way on this
little junket. Now, let me take a stab at this, Danny Boy. You're
supposed to be out here on a fact-finding mission for the
Judiciary boys, right? Dig up the dirt on Colonel John Creek,
leader of the Brethren and commander of the largest private militia in the country. Big Bad Wolf's suing the Federal Government
for millions, so they send your black ass out here to stir the pot.
Cause you got the fire in your belly, don'tcha, son? You'd just

love to be the one to string my hide up the Capitol flagpole. Oh, but you figured a night of fun at your buddy's love shack over in Sun Valley would help take the edge off so you called up your little suck-pump in Vegas and sent the company jet to pick her up. But now there's no more company jet, no Miss Candy and no political future for you when the shit hits the fan. Oh, Danny Boy. Your are in the crapper.

Wicked Games

Paul Boakye

Scene: the UK and Ghana

Serio-comic
Kofi: a British social worker, mixed race, 31

Here, Kofi stops by the beauty salon where his pregnant lover, Lyn works. As she washes his hair, Kofi entertains her with a story of a recent encounter with a new South African client.

KOFI: Babes, I've had a hard day too. You should see this woman I just met. Mad as a Hatter. I went to the house rang on the bell and I couldn't believe it when this woman opened the door. I just stood there in shock. I said, "Rose?…Rose Hoskins? Hello, I'm Kofi Ashampong, Hackney Social Services. I understand you've not been feeling too well. Said you've been hearing voices. I mean, can I come in? She just laid straight into me. *(Kofi acts out Rose's rage complete with her thick South African accent and hard piercing bug eyes. His transformation is total and scary.)* "What? Why? Why didn't they send me a woman? I told them to send me a woman! I don't want to see any men whatsoever! What do you men understand? It's this place it drives me mad. I should be back home where I belong in South Africa…"

(Lyn looks at Kofi's reflection in the mirror and recoils in horror.)

[LYN: Oh Jesus, Kofi, stop it! You're scaring me.]

KOFI: Babes, it freaked me out. *(Whispers.)* This woman was white South African but it was like someone had coated her skin black. I just wanted to wipe off her face. I couldn't believe it. She doesn't leave the house. People look at her and laugh. She was born from white South African parents but her great grandmother was a black woman raped by a Dutch white man. Her two sisters are white but somehow she just turned out jet black.

[LYN: You play the part very well.]

KOFI: You should have seen her. It's like the sins of the father visited upon the off-spring.

Wicked Games

Paul Boakye

Scene: the UK and Ghana

Dramatic
Leo: a sports instructor, black, 34

> *Leo has recently discovered that his close male friend, Kofi,
> harbors romantic feelings for him. Here, Leo muses on his
> tendency to give the wrong impression to other men with
> Kofi's female lover, Lyn.*

LEO: People always think because I'm friendly, I'm flirting. Or I'm
into them sexually. With my best friend Mark when he went mad,
and it literally happened like that *(Snaps fingers.)* I was there. I
had a hard time with him and it shattered the beliefs I had in our
friendship. I still stuck by him. And now he's out of hospital he
doesn't remember that day. He doesn't remember anything he
said. Or did, and I've just got to blank it out myself. I still think
hard about what I say to him. Try not to upset him. Make sure I'm
not being more physical to his girlfriend Tina than he thinks I
should be. Or that I'm giving her more attention or whatever.
Although Tina was my friend before he was. We were lovers
twelve years ago. But he came into the eternal triangle six years
ago…and It worries him that she'll always take my side—except
where he comes first. But I think that's a mean way of thinking.
When I met him he was doing nothing. I sorted him out. Got him
a flat in Holland Park. Introduced him to Tina. But he just feels
there's part of her that he can't have. But that's true of everyone
though. I mean, the way you talk to people never mirrors what
you're really thinking inside.

Windshook

Mary Gallagher

Scene: the Catskills

Dramatic
Rafe: a disillusioned vet, 20

> *Rafe has returned home from the Gulf War only to discover that his father has sold the land that he intended to farm. Devastated, Rafe moves onto the site of an old hunting camp where he makes his home in a tent. Here, he tells a visiting friend about the first time he went deer hunting with his father.*

RAFE: First time my dad took me hunting, we came up here to camp, the two of us, and we took our guns and went deep into the woods and sat on a big rock, holding our guns, and ready. And we sat. Seemed like hours. Dad didn't move a muscle, so I didn't either. Got real hungry, had to piss bad—but I didn't move. Then I seen her, a big, pretty doe coming toward us maybe thirty yards away, coming through the brush and walking straight at us, with that almost floating look they got on them twiggy legs, but you can see the strength in 'em too…Dad, he didn't move. And then I seen another doe behind her, and another…coming toward us in a line, like we'd called 'em to us. But Dad still didn't move. I was getting wild inside, sweating through my clothes— wild to get a clear shot while I could, while I had at least a chance of getting my first deer, showing Dad what I could do. But he was so still, I couldn't even feel his breathing, up close against him like I was, and I couldn't do nothing but what he would do…till there was thirteen doe coming toward us, and the closest one I swear was gonna come right up to me and nuzzle me for sugar…and Dad still didn't move. And then he moved so quick, I hadn't hardly felt him move 'fore I heard his gun crack out and seen that big

119

buck fall—that big six-pointer coming at the end of the line of doe, like Dad knowed he would do. He got him. I seen him fall. Them doe were scattering everywhere, and we just watched 'em go, and I said, "You got him, Dad!" And my dad said, "Well, I did, didn't I?"...After that...I was wild to go hunting...hunting with my dad.

Windshook

Mary Gallagher

Scene: the Catskills

Dramatic
Rafe: a disillusioned vet, 20

> *Rafe is determined to buy back the land his father sold. To that end he takes a job as a prison guard. Here, he describes his state of affairs.*

RAFE: When you go inside the gate, they lock the gate behind you. And when you go inside a door, they lock the door behind you. Pretty soon you're locked so far inside, it's like being underground. And you can't get out. You think about the air a lot. Feels like there ain't enough. Thousands of men inside them walls, and it's all sealed up. Locked windows with bars on 'em, and all them tight-locked doors. And the ceiling's pressing down on you, like you're miles down underground. Feels like it's hard to breathe. When your shift's over, they let you free for that little while. But the whole time you're outside, sucking in the clean air and looking at the sky, you got this tightness in your chest and this pressure above your eyes like something pressing down on you, 'cause you gotta go back. You don't wanta go to sleep, 'cause that'll bring the time closer when you'll walk through them gates again. And you do, you got to. Every time you hear them locks start to turn behind you, you want to scream out something and hurl them doors open and run. But you can't. You're in there, you're living in there, like the cons. Only difference is, they know when they're getting out. 'Cause you gotta stay in there long enough to buy your farm. And ain't no way of knowing yet how long that'll be.

Working Class

Richard Hoehler

Scene: a funeral home

Dramatic
A Man: Paying his respects at a friend's funeral, 30s

Here, a friend describes his relationship with the deceased.

(A man is standing alone onstage. A small red ribbon is pinned on his blazer.)

MAN: They told us to wait out here. That just the immediate family is in there payin their respects right now. I remember when my father died, that was the worst part—the immediate family. Got a little better when strangers started showin up. Least you could bitch about 'em without feeling guilty. *(Looks around.)* You know those people you never seen in your life—who come up and shake your hand and say, "I'm sorry." Why do people say that? I'm sorry. No…kiddin', Sherlock, everybody's sorry or they wouldn't be here. *(Pulls a plain white envelope out of his inside breast pocket.)* I just want to give them this and get back to work. I'm supposed to be there… *(Looks at watch.)* right now. *(Beat.)* They said it's okay to give money, you know like you really should, when it's the father or you know the head of the house… *(Putting the envelope back in his pocket.)* that's what people gave us… *(Beat.)* He was just this truck driver who came into the coffee shop I work in everyday and you know we talked…kidded around. Buttered roll with extra butter and a cup of regular—'like him.' *(Smiles.)* Days he was hungover he ordered a cherry coke before he even got to the counter. Said he had a buncha kids and they drove him to drink. You could tell he didn't really mean it. You could tell he liked his kids. My father didn't like kids. You can tell when somebody does. Red. That's what everybody called him. I don't know why. Cause his hair wasn't red. And the little sign outside in the lobby says Harold Fitzgerald, Sr. How the heck do you get Red out of that? I thought his last name would have something red in it, you know? That's how guys usually get those names. Get this. He called me "Irish." Cause he said I had the map of Ireland on my face. I'm not even one-fiftieth Irish. My last name is Kofman, for God's sake. But Red was an excellent tipper, so if he liked thinkin I was Irish, hey, I was Irish. When my boss told him I collected two dollar bills, he left one as a tip almost every other Friday when he got paid. *(Taps breast pocket.)* There's almost thirty of them in here. *(Beat.)* Some of the other guys who come in the shop, well...sometimes they give me a hard time...cause...well, I'm not married...and...I never know the football scores...or even who's playin...not that that alone should mean...But...still...they've figured out what the deal is. They do stuff like send these young college kids over to the counter and ask did I want to go to the drive-in or some crap. Then they all clink their glasses with their forks, you know like at weddings? Stupid stuff. It never happened when Red was there. I mean, nobody screwed around when he was at the counter. It was weird. And nice, you know? Kinda like...havin a break while you're still working. I don't know. At first I even wondered, you know, like maybe...you know how sometimes even though guys are married and all, they still...I remember he used to always go like *(Demonstrates squeezing his shoulder.) this* to me when he was leavin...but just friendly I guess...Nothin really...I woulda known if it was...No. Red was...straight. I mean, he used to get real corny all the time about marriage and kids and all. He was just a nice guy. Nice lookin' too, you know? The first day he did- n't show up I figured he was "under the eaves" again—that's the Irish way of sayin wickedly hung over. I was all ready the next morning with an extra strength cherry coke. But when he didn't come in for the rest of the week, I asked one of the other drivers from his outfit and he told me that Red was in the hospital 'big time' and that's all anybody knew. I thought about going to visit him...you know with a buttered roll and cup of regular. I even looked around for a card that had the map of Ireland on it. I couldn't find one. But...I didn't feel it was my place. Like people at the hospital would wonder who I was...to Red...maybe even get the wrong idea. That's all I need, you know for his wife to think... *(Beat.)* It's hard to do what you think you should do. Like as soon as you think you know what to do, there's always some reason not do it. *(Pause, looks around.)* But I made it here. Guess you gotta die to get any attention in this town. *(He turns around and looks upstage, pulls out envelope.)* They're going in now. God. I don't know what to say to these people. To his wife. Should I explain about the money? Or just give it to them and go? Should I tell them I'm just the waiter from the coffee shop he came into everyday and...I don't know. *(Beat.)* Should I say that Red made me smile every morning at 7:30 when I didn't feel like smiling and made me laugh and forget about the crap in my life for a little while and kept people off my case for a little while and that's why I'm here? You see the thing is, I don't want to sound like everybody else. Because I really am sorry.

(Music. He walks upstage slowly as lights fade. Blackout.)

profit organization serving playwrights). Reprinted by Permission of the Author. Inquiries: S. P. Miskowski, 1122 East Pike, Suite 950, Seattle, WA 98122-3934

Fragments Copyright © 1996 by John J. Garrett. Reprinted by Permission of the Author. Inquiries: Andrew Miano, William Morris Agency, 151 El Camino, Beverly Hills, CA 90212

Gangster Apparel Copyright © 1996 by Richard Vetere. Reprinted by Permission of the Author. Inquiries: Mary Meagher, William Morris Agency, 1325 Avenue of the Americas, New York, NY 10036

The Good Luck Charm Copyright © 1997 by James M. O'Donoghue. Reprinted by Permission of the Author. Inquiries: Doug Michael, The Frieda Fishbein Agency, Box 723, Bedford, NY 10506, (914) 234-7232, fishbein@juno.com

The Handyman Copyright © 1997 by Ronald Harwood. Reprinted by Permission of Faber & Faber. Inquiries: Judy Daish Associates — London

Happy Anniversary, Punk! Copyright © 1997 by Michael Ajakwe, Jr. Reprinted by Permission of the Author. Inquiries: Dytman & Associates, 9200 Sunset Blvd., Suite 809, Los Angeles, CA 90069

Have It All Copyright © 1995 by Robert Coles. Reprinted by Permission of the Author. Inquiries: Robert Coles, 80 Warren Street, New York, NY 10007

Hawk Dreaming Copyright © 1995 by Frank Cossa. Reprinted by Permission of the Author. Inquiries: Frank Cossa, 622 East 20th Street, IH, New York, NY 10009

How To Go Out On A Date In Queens Copyright © 1996 by Richard Vetere. Reprinted by Permission of the Author. Inquiries: Mary Meagher, William Morris Agency, 1325 Avenue of the Americas, New York, NY 10036

Infrared Copyright © 1995 by Mac Wellman. Reprinted by permission of the Author. Inquiries: Mitch Douglas, ICM, 40 West 57th Street, New York, NY 10019

Jack and Jill Copyright © 1995 by Alexander Speer. Reprinted by Permission of the Author. Professionals and amateurs are hereby warned that *Jack and Jill* is subject to a royalty. It is fully protected under the copyright laws of the United States of America and of all the countries covered by the International Copyright Union (including the Dominion of Canada and the rest of the British Commonwealth), and of all countries covered by the Pan American Copyright Convention and the Universal Copyright Convention, and of all countries with which the United States has reciprocal copyright copyright relations. All rights, including professional, amateur, motion picture, television, and allied rights, recitation, lecturing, public reading, radio broadcast, all other means of mechanical or electronic reproduction including CD-ROM and CD-I, information storage and retrieval systems and photocopying and the rights of translation into foreign languages, are strictly reserved. In its present form, the play is dedicated to the reading public only. Inquiries: Samuel French, 45 West 25th Street, New York, NY 10010

The John Doe Variations Copyright © 1996 by Silas Jones. Reprinted by Permission of the Author. Inquiries: Silas Jones, 642 Burnside Avenue #2, Los Angeles, CA 90036

King Gordogan by Radovan Ivsic. Translated by Roger Cardinal. American Version by Allan Graubard. Copyright © 1997 by Radovan Ivsic. Reprinted by Permission of the Author. Inquiries: Radovan Ivsic, 11 Rue de Mazagran, 75010 Paris, France

The Lady With The Toy Dog by Sari Bodi. Based Upon "The Lady With the Toy Dog" by Anton Checkov. Copyright © 1997 by Sari Bodi. Reprinted by Permission of the Author. Inquiries: Sari Bodi, 45 Hills Point Road, Westport, CT 06880

Smith and Kraus *Books For Actors*
THE MONOLOGUE SERIES
The Best Men's / Women's Stage Monologues of 1995
The Best Men's / Women's Stage Monologues of 1994
The Best Men's / Women's Stage Monologues of 1993
The Best Men's / Women's Stage Monologues of 1992
The Best Men's / Women's Stage Monologues of 1991
The Best Men's / Women's Stage Monologues of 1990
One Hundred Men's / Women's Stage Monologues from the 1980s
2 Minutes and Under: Character Monologues for Actors
Street Talk: Character Monologues for Actors
Uptown: Character Monologues for Actors
Ice Babies in Oz: Character Monologues for Actors
Monologues from Contemporary Literature: Volume I
Monologues from Classic Plays
100 Great Monologues from the Renaissance Theatre
100 Great Monologues from the Neo-Classical Theatre
100 Great Monologues from the 19th C. Romantic and Realistic Theatres
A Brave and Violent Theatre: 20th C. Irish Monologues, Scenes &
             Historical Context
Kiss and Tell: Restoration Monologues, Scenes and Historical Context
The Great Monologues from the Humana Festival
The Great Monologues from the EST Marathon
The Great Monologues from the Women's Project
The Great Monologues from the Mark Taper Forum
SCENE STUDY SERIES
Scenes From Classic Plays 468 B.C. to 1960 A.D.
The Best Stage Scenes of 1995
The Best Stage Scenes of 1994
The Best Stage Scenes of 1993
The Best Stage Scenes of 1992
The Best Stage Scenes for Men / Women from the 1980s
YOUNG ACTOR SERIES
Great Scenes and Monologues for Children
Great Monologues for Young Actors
Great Scenes for Young Actors
Multicultural Monologues for Young Actors
Multicultural Scenes for Young Actors

If you require pre-publication information about upcoming Smith and Kraus
books, you may receive our semi-annual catalogue, free of charge, by sending
your name and address to *Smith and Kraus Catalogue, P.O. Box 127, Lyme, NH
03768. Or call us at (603) 922-5118, fax (603) 922-3348.*